Unde

Internet

Other Titles of Interest

BP404	*How to create pages for the Web using HTML - 2nd edition*
BP420	E-Mail on the Internet
BP433	Your Own Web Site on the Internet
BP435	Programming in C++
BP453	*How to search the World Wide Web efficiently*
BP477	Using Microsoft FrontPage 2000
BP483	*Fun Web pages with JavaScript*
BP488	Internet Explorer 5 explained
BP490	Web Pages Using Microsoft Office 2000
BP494	Basic Internet Skills
BP499	Java Programming explained
BP500	Java 2 Programming explained
BP501	*XHTML & CSS explained*
BP503	Using Dreamweaver 4
BP504	Using Flash 5
BP507	Easy Internet Troubleshooting

Titles in italics are by John Shelley

Understanding the Internet

by

John Shelley

BERNARD BABANI (publishing) LTD
THE GRAMPIANS
SHEPHERDS BUSH ROAD
LONDON W6 7NF
ENGLAND

www.babanibooks.com

PLEASE NOTE

Although every care has been taken with the production of this book to ensure that any projects, designs, modifications and/or programs, etc., contained herewith, operate in a correct and safe manner and also that any components specified are normally available in Great Britain, the Publishers and Author(s) do not accept responsibilty in any way for the failure (including fault in design) of any project, design, modification or program to work correctly or to cause damage to any equipment that it may be connected to or used in conjunction with, or in respect of any other damage or injury that may be so caused, nor do the Publishers accept responsibility in any way for the failure to obtain specified components.

Notice is also given that if equipment that is still under warranty is modified in any way or used or connected with home-built equipment then that warranty may be void.

First Published - January 2002

British Library Cataloguing in Publication Data

A catalogue record for this book is available from the British Library

ISBN 0 85934 517 3

Cover Design by Gregor Arthur

Printed and Bound in Great Britain by Guernsey Press

Preface

I first wrote about the Internet some five years ago when it was known as the Information Superhighway. There was much hype and speculation about how it was set to change the way Society would communicate. Education for all, shopping, banking and entertainment would all be "on the Net". Today, Society has taken a more sober view of the Internet.

The amount of information available has increased dramatically and, fortunately, so has its quality. E-mail has become part of everyday office life, some would say a chore. Intranets abound and the number of people creating and maintaining web pages has grown astronomically. Indeed, for many, it has become a job requirement akin to word processing skills. Search engines have improved their keyword search techniques so that, if it is out there, you stand a good chance of finding it, eventually.

This book looks at how the Internet and the World Wide Web has developed over the past few years and discusses some of the latest technologies and how they may affect our lives. For those who missed it the first time around, we explain how the Internet works and introduce many of the jargon terms which crop up even in everyday conversation.

I would like to thank JANET for permission to include their Backbone illustration on page 58 and list their URL:

`http://www.ja.net/`

John Shelley, September, 2001.

Trademarks

Microsoft, Microsoft Windows, Internet Assistant, Internet Explorer, FrontPage, Outlook, Word are registered trademarks of Microsoft Corporation. The clipart used in some illustrations has been taken from the Clipart Gallery of Word 97.

Unix is a registered trademark of AT&T.

About, AOL, AskJeeves, Alta Vista, Associated London Metro Ltd., CIO, Cyber Patrol, Dreamweaver, Eudora, Netnanny, Netscape, Opera, howstuffworks, Netcraft, Steetmap UK, Webshots, Search Engine Watch, Internet.com, Yahoo!, Google, ZDNet, Northern Light, Queryserver, Vivisimo, Pegasus, Hotmail, TalkCity, SurfMonkey are registered trademarks or copyrights of their relevant organisations.

References to the various URLs on the Internet and extracts from various sites are acknowledged here.

All other trademarks are the registered and legally protected trademarks of the companies who make the products. There is no intent to use the trademarks generically and readers should investigate ownership of a trademark before using it for any purpose.

Contents

ONE:

Introduction to the Internet & the WWW

The Internet & WWW have been around for some time and most people have at least a vague idea of what it can do. Not the same when I wrote a similar book some five years ago.

There has been much hype and hope but there has been a great deal of disappointment. It has not turned out to be quite the panacea first intended, not to mention the fate of the `dot.coms`.

Has it worked?
This text takes a positive approach because behind all the failures there have been many successes. The failures can be seen simply to prove that it was in its infancy. Dreams are a vision of what may be, of what is possible. Reality is never quite the same thing.

One of the original claims of TV, was education for all. But reality has shown that some programmes can be very good (drama, sport, educational) but some are appalling. The technology cannot be blamed for this. Likewise the Internet cannot be blamed when it is used for dubious purposes, such as porn, or the fact that e-business has not taken off as expected.

Many developments have recently taken place which are set to change the way in which we access information. The WWW is still a major force for exchanging information, if it is designed well.

1: Introduction

Since I first wrote about this subject, the Internet has had to be policed, new laws introduced and people are learning to become more responsible for how they use the Internet.

Internet or WWW or does it matter?
Is it necessary to make a distinction between the two? I think it is. The Internet is the physical technology which passes information around. Like a telephone system is used to pass voice data. What is actually passed around is the information. Thus, if I say, "Send me an e-mail.", the message is the information but the message is sent over the Internet. The Internet is a term for accessing all the information stored in the World Wide Web.

The basis for the Web is the Internet. The WWW makes use of many of the mechanisms which the Internet provides. The Web needs the Internet but the Internet does not need the Web. Indeed, it existed before the WWW. The more technical aspects of how the Internet works are discussed in Chapter 8.

In the following Chapters, we shall discuss:

- the type of information available
- where the WWW came from
- means of information exchange (e-mail, newsgroups, chat rooms, instant messaging, and so forth)
- how to find information
- where the Internet came from
- how the Internet works
- how to create your own web pages
- the future - where it is going
- some social and moral issues

In the next Chapter, we shall discuss the sort of information we can access.

TWO:

Information

The Web is awash with all sorts of information, some good, some bad, some indifferent. It can come in a variety of formats, text, images, sound, videos as well as interactivity. On page 5, taken from the About Network!, you can see that there is everything from Arts/Literature to Autos/Pets and from Religion to TV/Radio. It is rather like a combination of many different magazines. We can also use search engines to find informative articles, for example about medical conditions, news articles from many of the world's leading newspapers, stock exchange updates, specifications about new web languages, and much more.

When I was searching for MCTD (multiple connective tissue disorder) for someone, the person eventually knew more about it than her consultant. (A bit worrying!) Some GPs are becoming concerned that their patients have more specific knowledge about their own illnesses than they do. Whereas others actually approve of this, since instead of the doctor being the fount of all knowledge, they can have a dialogue with their patients, aiding and directing them towards a particular course of treatment.

The Internet will affect how doctors and patients interact. There are some 100,000 web health sites. But be careful, some are peddling old wives tales and their information is sometimes not researched, anecdotal and even bogus.

But what about the quality of the information? Is it any good? I am reminded of a comment made by Andrew Alexander of the Daily Mail back in 1996

> *"The complaint a generation or two ago was that specialisation was leading people to know more and more about less and less. The new generation of anoraks will know less and less about more and more ... I shall hold out for a while yet."*

Has he been proved to be correct? That is really for you to decide. Essentially, it depends on how well you can use the WWW to find information. Some people, especially professional researchers, are highly experienced in choosing the right sort of search engine. We shall look at this point in Chapter 6.

For the moment, we shall discuss:

- what the WWW is
- where it came from
- how to use it to find information

What is the WWW and why is it so popular?

From your own desktop and at the click of a button you can access web sites from anywhere in the world. A whole range of different types of information can be retrieved: text, images, audio and video. There are forms for shopping, surveys, registration details, tax and many other examples. If you have ever filled in a search engine *search-box* with keywords then you are using a form.

Here is the address of the About web site on page 5:

`http://a-zlist.about.com/num.htm`

or try this for their home page:

`http://home.about.com/`

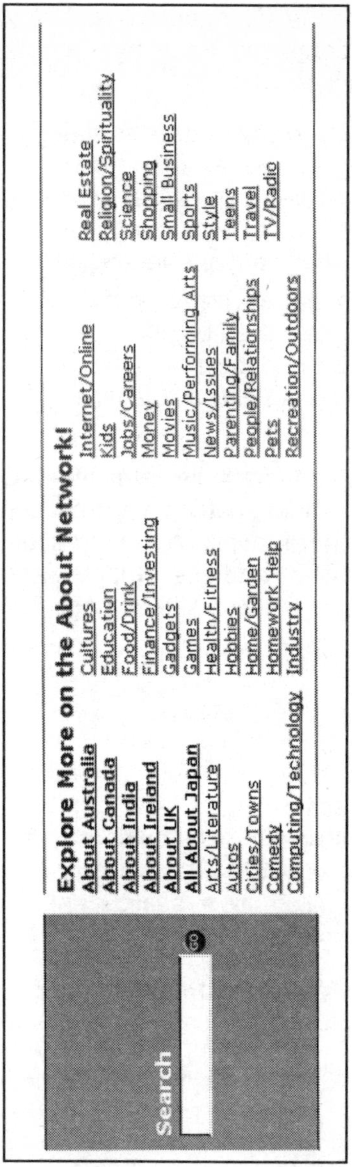

Search

Go

Explore More on the About Network!

About Australia	Cultures	Internet/Online	Real Estate
About Canada	Education	Kids	Religion/Spirituality
About India	Food/Drink	Jobs/Careers	Science
About Ireland	Finance/Investing	Money	Shopping
About UK	Gadgets	Movies	Small Business
All About Japan	Games	Music/Performing Arts	Sports
Arts/Literature	Health/Fitness	News/Issues	Style
Autos	Hobbies	Parenting/Family	Teens
Cities/Towns	Home/Garden	People/Relationships	Travel
Comedy	Homework Help	Pets	TV/Radio
Computing/Technology	Industry	Recreation/Outdoors	

This is from the About® index page.

It provides information specific to six countries apart from its own list of topics.

You can either click on one of the topics or type a search phrase into the Search box.

Note that web pages are continually changing, this was current at the time of writing.

2: Information

Why so Popular?

Millions are using it every day for e-mail and for finding information.

- it is easy to use - you do not need to be a computer nerd
- you can access the web from any place (home, office, Internet kiosks, etc.)
- it provides a whole range of types of information
- it is easy to create web pages (once you look at Chapter 9 you too can create a Web page)
- there is a great deal of published material
- the information is improving in quality all the time

How the Web is used today

Many of the following topics are available from the CIO Web Central site. A few of their main categories are listed below to indicate the wealth of available information. Simply type the following web address, (upper and lowercase is significant) to get to the web site on page 7.

`http://www.cio.com/WebMaster/sem2_how.html`

By companies all over the World:

- for external communication...
- to share product information
- to learn about the marketplace
- to share in process work with business partners
- and for internal sharing of information...
- by business people...
- for education at all levels...
- by technical people...
- for reference information ... want to know the source of a quotation, similar words, distance from one place to another, time zones
- for online news... where did that newspaper topic come from
- to provide financial information...

- by lawyers...
- for library information...
- for government information...
- for personal services...
- and for information about the Web itself!
- and for some unusual reasons...

Each category is a link to other web pages. If you are new to browser searching, it may take a little practice working your way around, but with practice you gain experience

Browsers - How to find such information

A browser is the technical term for a program which can find any web page on the Internet and display it on your screen. Netscape and Internet Explorer (IE) are two of the most popular.

We have already looked at the *About.com* site. Here is a truly excellent site which we look at below for those interested in reference material on law, education, etc.

Fortunately, we do not need to know much in order to use a browser. We simply click various buttons and it does the rest.

The above shows Internet Explorer, the Microsoft browser. The top line is called the *Title Bar* giving the title of the Web page (*How the Web is used...*) followed by the name of the browser. The second line is the *Menu Bar* with the *File*, *Edit*, *View*, etc., menus. The third line is the *Standard Buttons Bar* allowing you to go *Back* to a previous page or *Forward* to another page which has already been opened and displayed. The *Stop* button allows you to interrupt and stop the loading of a page which you have asked to be displayed. Usually, this is clicked when the time to display the page is becoming excessive. The other buttons are mentioned below.

The fourth line is called the *Address Bar*. It is where you can type in the address of the Web page you wish to display. It is called a Uniform Resource Locator (URL and discussed in detail below). You need to know the exact address otherwise the page will not be found, rather like sending a letter to someone's home - you must know the person's correct address. The rest of the window is where the page is actually displayed. Scroll bars will appear if the window cannot display all the information.

Most browsers have a similar set-up. Here is Netscape's approach. Notice that the *Stop* button is at the far right and that *Bookmarks* is the same as *Favorites* in Internet Explorer and again is in a different position. The *Forward* and *Stop* buttons are grey indicating that there is no forward page to select and since the page has been displayed totally, the loading (displaying) process is complete and therefore the *Stop* button is inactive (grey).

If you have been given or found a URL such as the following:

`http://www.cio.com/WebMaster/sem2_how.html`

you would type it into the *Address Bar* location box and press the Enter key. The browser would do everything necessary to find and display the page.

URL (Uniform Resource Locator)

A complete URL consists of:

- the *method* by which a document is accessed
- the unique address of the *site* (server) where the document is held
- the name of the document - *file name*

Example:

`http://www.ic.ac.uk/courses.htm`

`http` is the Web's own method for accessing and transferring documents between different Web servers. It stands for the ***h***yper***t***ext ***t***ransfer ***p***rotocol. It is a set of rules (the *protocol*) used by network servers for transmitting data.

`://` is a separator marking off the transmission protocol from the rest of the URL

`www.ic.ac.uk` is the site address of where the document is stored, and refers to the Web server (*www*) at Imperial College (*ic*) which is part of the academic community (*ac*) in the United Kingdom (*uk*). Each site has its own unique Web site address, just like every household has its own unique postal address or telephone number. Indeed, the site address *is* a set of four numbers each separated by a full stop. This is why you may sometimes see numbers rather than letters in some URLs: `http://123.45.06.78/`

Names are easier to type and to remember rather than numbers. The names used are converted to numbers by the Web server. It is similar to looking up a telephone number for a given name.

`courses.htm` is the actual file name of the Web page held in the server's storage discs.

Frequently, between the web site address and the actual document that you want to look at, there may be many folders and sub-folders. For example:

http://www.abc.com/folderx/sub-folderx/page.htm

Today, most browsers will assume the `http://` if it is left off, thus: www.abc.com/folderx/sub-folderx/page.htm is assumed to be the same as the above.

Web Site: The term *web site* can be confusing. Sometimes it is used to refer to an actual web server which stores web pages which anyone can visit and obtain copies.

At other times it is used to refer to an actual web page itself. We need to see in what context it is being used.

You may like to try the CIO link given above and try some of the categories. Here is the list of topics displayed when the *by lawyers* link was clicked:

Categories:

Computer Law
General Sources
Libraries and References
U.S.

Canadian
Germany
Israel
New Zealand
United Kingdom
Laws
Publications
Law Firms
Articles
Telnet and Gopher Sites

Each category has its own list of links. Information on the Web is often on an index page which has a variety of links to more detailed information.

It is easy to get lost, but some effort has gone into making it more simple. The following is becoming a common navigational aid:

<<Previous Page | Next Page>> Title of Current Page

Here some of the categories *for reference Information*:

Words

Bartlett's Familiar Quotations
Elements of Style, By William Strunk, Jr
On-Line Dictionaries Page - a list of online dictionaries
Roget's Thesaurus
WWWebster Dictionary
OneLook - searches 81 dictionaries

It also includes many other references including a world clock, facts, travel, dictionaries and much more.

The following has been modified to fit this book.

2: Information

Distance

How Far is it? - find the distance between cities

Money

The Universal Currency Converter
Currency Converter

Place

Area Code Lookup
Area/City/Country Code Phone Lookup Service
Geographic Name Server by City or ZIP code

etc., etc.

I used the *distance* link to find the distance and map for a trip from London to Newcastle. I had to type in London, UK and Newcastle, UK since the link is weighted in favour of the States. Here is what it gave me (after asking which Newcastle I wanted, very smart!):

Please choose one, or re-enter your query:

Newcastle, England, United Kingdom

Location: 53:01:00N 2:14:00W

Newcastle upon Tyne, England, United Kingdom

Location: 54:59:17N 1:37:10W

I also tried out the directions and was astonished to be given an incredibly detailed set. It is well worth a try.

A few years ago, one could not have expected such information but over time, the amount and detail of the information has been improving.

To think, I was using a USA link but it was smart enough to show me (if I included UK in the town name) how to get from London (UK) to Newcastle (UK).

Distance result: Distance between London, England, United Kingdom and Newcastle, England, United Kingdom, as the crow flies:

138 miles (222 km) (120 nautical miles)

Initial heading from London to Newcastle:
northwest (320.3 degrees)
Initial heading from Newcastle to London:
southeast (138.6 degrees)

See **driving distance and directions** (courtesy MapBlast).

See these places on the map (courtesy Xerox PARC).

London, England, United Kingdom

Location: 51:30:00N 0:07:00W

Newcastle, England, United Kingdom

Location: 53:01:00N 2:14:00W

Bookmarks/Favorites (US spelling)

Browsers allow readers to mark a site as a Bookmark or Favorite. The reader can then select this from a list rather than having to retype (and remember) sites you would like to revisit. Here is an example from Internet Explorer. The list of my favourite sites are shown on the left after I had clicked the Favorites button. Note the scroll bar to display more sites.

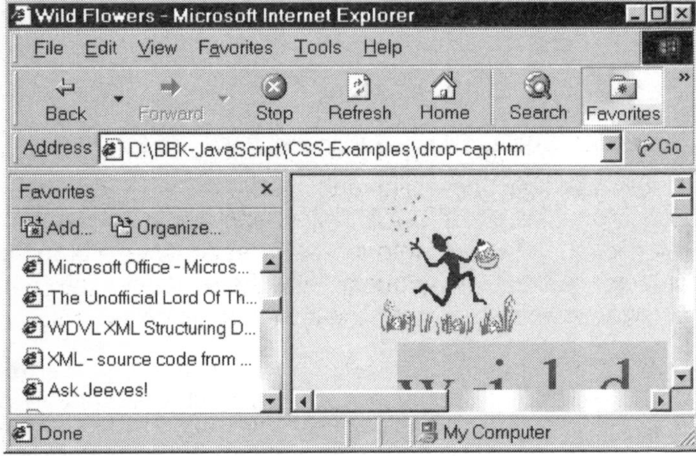

THREE:

The WWW - where did it come from?

The growth of the WWW has been phenomenal. No one really knows how big it is. In 1996, it was estimated that there were over 60 million people on the Internet, today some 500 million people are logging on and off all the time. In May 2001, Netcraft survey reported some 30 million sites:
`http://www.netcraft.com/survey/`

The original concept of the WWW was to allow researchers at CERN, a High Energy Physics establishment, to share project data and information with others working on similar projects world-wide. But there was a problem since each project site would be using its own local network. Unfortunately, each local computer network had its own language, and there was no easy way for one network to communicate with another network.

Now, one of the basic concepts behind the Internet was that there *should be* a common language. If each network agreed on this language, then they could 'talk' to each other. This 'talking' is really requests for particular files and a common transfer method. The Internet, which predates the WWW by some 30 years was the ideal vehicle for exchanging information. (See Chapter 8 for a discussion on the more technical details.) So it made sense for the WWW to be built upon the Internet and to make use of many of the mechanisms the Internet provides.

Tim Berners-Lee developed the basic ideas of the WWW to which others have since added. Those researchers involved in the WWW agreed to work by a set of common principles:

- there would be no central control, because people would work within the agreed guidelines. Anyone could publish and anyone with the proper authorisation would be able to read the information
- all networks in the system would use the same rules (protocols). These networks are what today we call web servers
- URLs would be used as the network-wide addressing system (see page 9)
- all Web browsers would use HTML as the basic language for marking up the information

Some of the advantages of creating web pages are:

- any number of people could get a copy
- only one original was required
- amendments could be made to an original and these would be instantly available to the whole world

> ***Protocol:***
> A protocol is simply a set of rules agreed by two or more parties. Anyone using the protocol will be able to understand what the other is 'talking' about. English grammar is a protocol, a set of rules whereby people can communicate with one another.
>
> Individual networks often have their own internal language which they understand but others cannot. When the Internet was originally designed and many different networks were involved some common language, a protocol, had to be created.

Web Servers & Web Clients

A web server is an organisation's computer which stores all the documents written in HTML for anyone to gain access to. Each server must have a unique address (just like every home in the UK) so that one server can contact another. Every retrievable piece of information on the Web has its own unique identity. This includes the name of the HTML document (or image or video), the web server on which it is stored and the particular protocol used to retrieve it, such as `http`. (See page 9.) All this information is called a Uniform Resource Locator (URL).

Browsers can retrieve documents which are stored on a web server. Usually, each document is created on a personal computer and then given to a Web Master/Manager who then puts it on the web server. The web master will also provide the complete URL of where that document is stored. By publishing the URL of that document (on your business card, adverts, e-mail signatures, letter headings, etc.) others will be able to locate your web documents.

A web server, then, is the computer which stores web documents and allows them to be retrieved by anyone connected to the Internet.

Web Client

A web client is what we know as the browser. A user of the browser program can request a copy of a web page in one of three ways:

- by entering the URL in the address location box
- by clicking on a hypertext link in an existing web page
- by using a search engine to find a list of URLs and selecting one of them

When any of the above is performed, the browser sends a request to the local web server to which it is attached. This web server will then contact the web server holding the document requested by the Client (your browser) via the

Internet. That server will return a copy of the requested document to your browser which will then be able to display it according to the HTML mark-up language.

We therefore have this idea of a Client-Server, whereby a browser will contact a server to request a particular document. Once the web document is sent back, the browser can display the web page. The client therefore performs two main duties. First of all, a request for a document and secondly the display of that document.

The language that web clients and web servers use to communicate with each other is the hypertext transfer protocol (`http`). All web clients and servers must be able to 'speak' `http` in order to send and receive web documents. (For the brave, web servers are sometimes referred to as HTTP servers or 'http daemons' - `httpd` servers.)

We must not confuse the `http` protocol with the IP addresses (see page 66). The `http` protocol is used to send IP addresses as well as what document to retrieve.

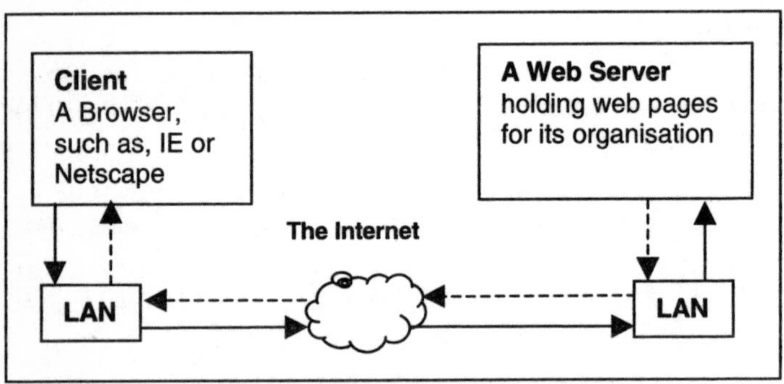

Figure 3.1: ***Solid lines*** **indicate Client's request to server**
Dashed lines **indicate server's response**

FOUR:

E-mail

Of all activities performed over the Internet, e-mail is the most common. In 1998, some 6.5 million messages a minute, were being sent in the USA alone, according to one marketing company. Electronic mailing (e-mail) has been around for much longer than the WWW. Once it was discovered, back in 1971, that a computer at one site could be linked to a computer at another site via the telephone system, people began sending messages to each other rather than use the time-consuming postal service. Like most technologies, however, what starts off as a 'good thing' can become degraded over time. But let us start with the positive aspects before mentioning some of the bad points.

Over the past 10 years, e-mail has become an integral part of the everyday life for many working people. Indeed, it has become an essential tool for human communication. It is less formal and faster than sending letters and is less intrusive than a telephone call and, of course, very cheap. Provided both the sender and the recipient are connected via the Internet, messages can be sent in seconds to anywhere in the world. This is how I was able to keep in touch with my daughter when she went on a 'gap year' to Mexico. We still made telephone calls, of course, since there is nothing like hearing someone's voice.

The first e-mail message was sent in 1971 by an engineer named Ray Tomlinson. Tomlinson is best remembered for the use of the @ sign (pronounced 'at') to designate the beginning of the address of the recipient's machine.

An e-mail message, even today, is nothing more than a simple text message, although *attachments* can be included by the modern e-mail programs. To send and receive messages an e-mail program, such as Eudora, Outlook Express, Microsoft Outlook or Pegasus, is required. People using free e-mail services, such as Hotmail or Yahoo, simply use an e-mail program which is displayed in a web page. But all of them have four basic functions and some have a few extra bells and whistles:

- displays a list of all messages sent to you and typically the message *header* which shows the date and time the message was sent
- allows you to select one of the messages and displays its content (the so-called *body* of the message)
- allows you to create and send new messages
- allows attachments to be included in your messages and displays any attachments you receive

How it works
You need an e-mail server which your e-mail program can contact. This may be owned by your organisation or you may link from home to one owned by an Internet Service Provider (ISP) for free or at a cost. Let us take an example of a company with its own e-mail server. The server is nothing more than a glorified PC with a huge hard disc and a few programs which perform the sending and the receiving of messages.

The first thing you need is an *account*. (If you buy things regularly from a particular store, you need an account. This is what an e-mail account is.) The account is a name given to you by the company, such as `jsmith` or `johndoe2`. It must be unique, so if there are two John

Doe's in a company, the second one may have the digit 2 appended to make his account unique. If you subscribe to an e-mail service, you will be invited to invent your own account name if it has not already been chosen by someone else. If it has, then the service provider will ask you to supply some other name (possibly by offering you a choice of similar names).

After the account and separated by the @ symbol, is the address of the e-mail server: `j.smith@abc.com`

The e-mail server will store a list of all authorised account names in its database. When someone in the organisation is sent a message, it compares the name with the names in its database. When that person connects to the e-mail server, the server will send all the new messages to that person's PC.

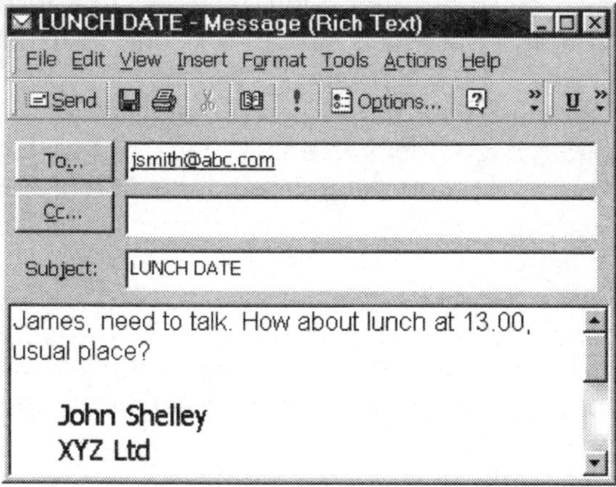

A typical 'new message' would look like the above, shown in Microsoft Outlook. Note that there is no *From* box. That will be added automatically to the recipient's message by the server since it knows who sent the message, together with the date and time, as shown below. Here is what the recipient will receive:

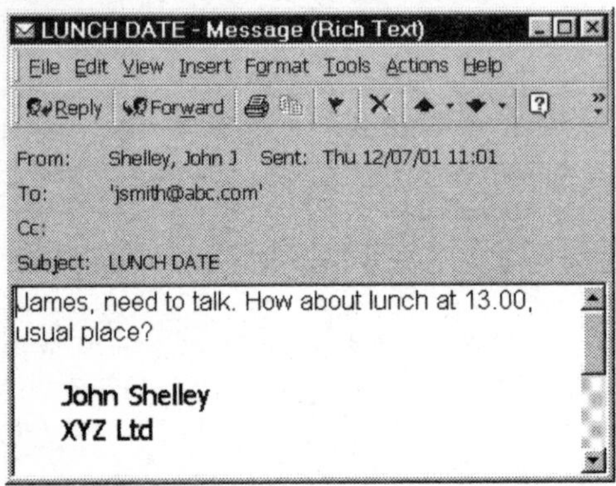

The Real E-Mail system

In practice, there are two e-mail servers, one to handle incoming mail - the POP3 server, and one to handle the outgoing mail - the SMTP server. Whenever you send an e-mail message, your e-mail program (officially called the *e-mail client*) has to complete four steps. Let us suppose that I am sending a message from `j.shelley@xyz.com` to `jsmith@abc.com`.

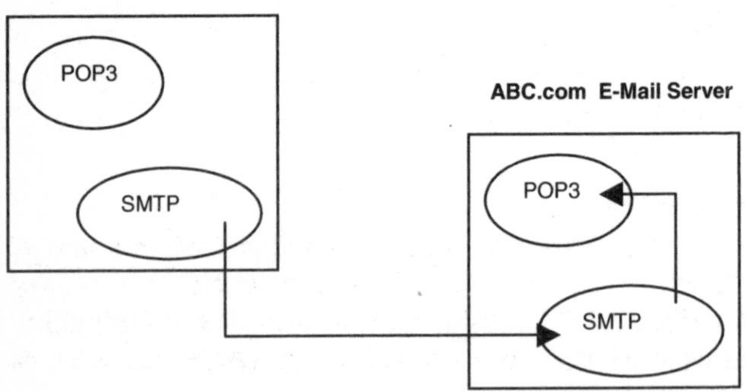

First, my e-mail client contacts the Simple Mail Transfer Protocol server at XYZ Ltd and passes it the address of the recipient, the address of the sender (me) and the body of the message. The SMTP server will recognise my account name as one of its valid users:

- it divides the recipient's address into the account name and the actual server address, using the @ symbol as the separator
- it now needs to connect to the `abc.com` SMTP server and pass over the account name of the recipient, the address of the sender, the body of the message plus the date and time the message was sent
- the `abc.com` server recognises `jsmith` as one of its own valid accounts, so it hands everything over to the POP3 server at `abc.com`
- when James Smith next logs on to his e-mail server, his POP3 server will deliver my message

On the previous page is a diagrammatic explanation of what is involved. POP3 stands for Post Office Protocol. If I were to send a message to someone else in my organisation, the SMTP server would recognise the recipient's account as one of its own, and would simply pass the details over to the POP3 server at XYZ Ltd.

If you are interested in exactly how the SMTP server at XYZ Ltd finds the address of the `abc.com` server, this technicality is discussed in Chapter 8 under *How the Internet Works.*

Adding Attachments

An e-mail message is only a simple text message. Suppose you want to send a spreadsheet file or a picture or a sound file? You would need to tell your e-mail client that you wish to include an attachment. The client will ask you for the name of the file and where it is stored on your computer's hard disc. Having supplied this information, the attached file will be sent to the recipient along with the original e-mail text message. The recipient would see something like this, Figure 4.1:

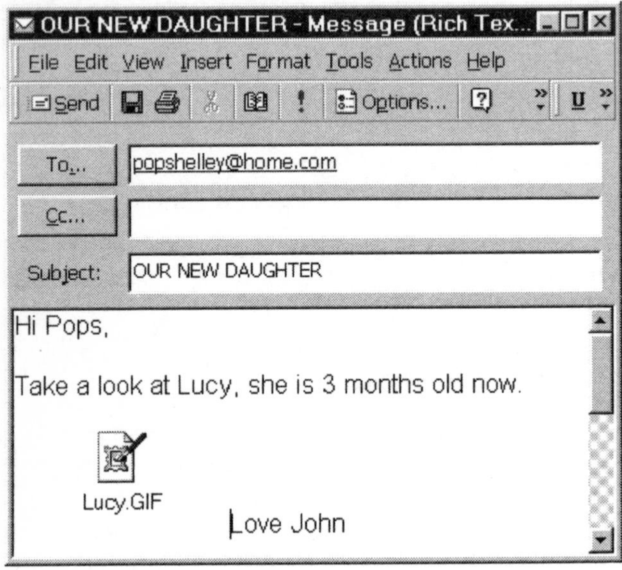

Figure 4.1: Sending an e-mail with an attachment

Granddad will receive the following but in order to view it, he must have the same program as the one in which it was created. Images can often be opened and viewed by almost any other image program, but Word documents, Excel files, sound files would require the recipient to have Word, Excel, etc., and possibly even the same version of the original program or a higher version. The recipient would simply double click the file icon (`Lucy.gif`) and provided the correct program is available on that machine, the program would be opened and the file displayed automatically.

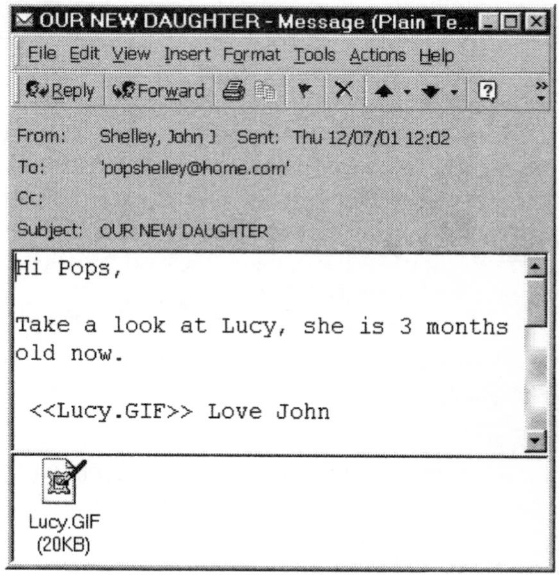

Figure 4.2: Receiving an attachment

Instant Messaging

When an e-mail message is sent, there is no way of knowing whether the recipient has read your message. If you want a reply, the recipient needs to perform three steps:

- read message
- click the *reply* to button
- send the message

Not a great task unless you want an instant reply. A variation on the basic e-mail is *instant messaging*, something comparatively new to many people but gaining in popularity. It is most effective when you need replies to messages here and now, instantly, with no delays, in what is called *real-time*. The world of stockbrokers and real-time news comes to mind, as well as very high profile company projects where all involved must respond now.

Let us suppose that you have a list of people you wish to interact with on a regular, instant and real-time basis. The interaction may take the form of text messages, sharing files, sounds, images, even talk, and so on. In November, 1996, a company called Mirablis, founded by four Israeli programmers, introduced ICQ, a free product that anyone could use. ICQ is pronounced 'I Seek You'. Mirablis was acquired by AOL in 1998 to become AOL Instant Messenger (AIM).

How it Works

Once the software is installed on your machine (and on the machines of all your contacts), you run the program. (Initially, you will have to supply a list of contacts, let us assume that has been done.)

The program contacts an ICQ server using a proprietary protocol called ICQ v5.

- you enter a username and password

Once those have been verified, your ICQ program sends your machine's Internet address and the addresses of those in your list of contacts to the ICQ server.

- the server now contacts everyone in the list to see whether they are connected (on-line)
- the ICQ server will send back a list of all those who are currently logged on to the ICQ program
- (each of the contacts will also have run their program to tell the server that they are on-line and each will

now be told by the ICQ server that you have just logged on)

- from the list of names, you can click one or more and send a message
- both your machine and your contacts' machines will open a new window with your message
- replies and any other messages will be added to this window (the window expands to show scroll bars)

You now have instant messaging - IM.

The messages which are sent do not go through the ICQ server, but directly to your contacts via the Internet addresses supplied. When you (or any of the contacts) wish to end the session, you simply close your ICQ program. This will effectively send a message back to the ICQ server, which will then inform all the remaining contacts that you have just disconnected and that you are unavailable. The messages are not stored or kept.

Currently, MNS Explorer and Yahoo! Messenger (amongst many others) include instant messaging services. Most systems have an encryption facility but you would be advised not to send confidential messages via IM.

An interesting alternative feature of most IM systems is that you can talk to your contacts provided all have a sound card, speakers and a microphone. Business users are beginning to find that IM allows them to have virtual conferences whereby they can collaborate easily on their projects. It is opening up a whole new world of communication. (Somewhat annoying for those taking a sneaky 'day off ill'.)

Pros and Cons of E-Mail

Pros:

We have covered many of the useful features of e-mail. One that we have not discussed is that you can set up a list of contacts and create a group name for the list. You invent the name and can easily add (or delete) individual members' e-mail addresses in the group list. When you want to send a message to all the people in the group, you simply type the message once and enter the group name into the To: box. The one message will be delivered to all members of the group.

Some companies will do this for you, such as eGroups:

`http://www.egroups.co.uk/`

It is a free service for small or large groups of people.

Cons:

But is my e-mail private, secure and what about viruses? E-mail is not private. Anyone receiving it can pass it on to all and sundry, as we all know from recent media reports. The message is stored on the e-mail server (for how long?) until it is deleted. Any administrator of the server can read any of the messages which are sent. Some organisations regularly spy on what is being sent and received. According to a recent survey, one in four employees has his/her Internet use watched by their employers. Surveillance software such as MIMEsweeper and Websense is used to scan e-mails and Internet use.

You have a choice. If the information you want to send is sensitive, then do not use e-mail or, at least, encrypt the message. It is better than getting the sack.

Legally, companies have the right to look at e-mails, unless they have agreed not to. So, as someone put it, do not put anything into an e-mail message which you would not be happy putting on a postcard.

Encryption:
This is a method for scrambling files, including e-mail messages. One of the most popular encryption programs is PGP (Pretty Good Privacy®). It is not an easy program to use, but there are more user-friendly versions available. For more information try:

`http://web.mit.edu/network/pgp.html`

`http://www.pgpi.org/`

Viruses:
It happened to me once. I was concentrating on writing a report when an e-mail appeared which invited me to click an attachment. Normally, I am ultra careful about opening any attachment from unknown sources. I mistook the From box for the To box and opened the wretched thing. It took an hour and profuse apologies before it was cleared up. No real damage was done but the virus looked at my Contacts list and sent them a copy (from me!). Many of my colleagues opened the attachment "I had sent" assuming I was a trusted source. It repeated itself (over a thousand times) in my Inbox until the e-mail server ground to a halt, overloaded with so many 'new' messages. Oh well!

Why did not my virus checker program warn me of the possible danger? It is a very sophisticated one and is updated regularly, but it was just *one* day too late. The moral is, if you have any doubt, never open an attachment. One trick is to look at the file extension. If it is unusual in any way, especially if it has an `.exe`, contact the sender before opening it. Even common extensions will not protect you since viruses can be spread by Word document macros, Excel macros, etc.

Too many e-mails
It is expected that many managers will be spending up to four hours a day sifting through their e-mails by 2002.

4: <u>E-mail</u>

Organisations are becoming increasingly alarmed about the amount of e-mail which is clogging up their network systems. Some are providing training in how to become more efficient in the use of e-mail. Many are promoting the use of instant messaging which is faster than e-mail and since the messages are not saved, less taxing on computer networks.

One final word. Spiteful e-mails attacking companies are usually circulated by individuals rather than by rival companies. But even if it is a lie, it can be half way around the world before the company can take steps to rectify the libel.

Text Messaging

Text messaging using mobile phones has become a recent craze fuelled mainly by teenagers. Now marketing managers want to take advantage of the short message service (SMS), it is apparently more personal than postal junk.

Promotions from a variety of sources, such as banks, financial companies, airlines, etc., could soon be sent direct to these handsets. Some mobile operators already send their customers details about new tariffs, promotions and competitions. Airlines may want to inform people in, say, Manchester that there are 30 spare seats on a flight to Orlando at a certain price. Broadcasters use it to send out trailers for shows.

One of the features, of the text messaging, which worries some teaching staff is the use of acronyms as a shorthand for speed and to convey more information in a limited space. Could you recognise this?

`2B or nt 2B, that is the ?`

An *emoticon* (also known as a "smiley") is a symbol composed of a few text characters, and used as a kind of emotional shorthand to add meaning to a message.

They have to be viewed sideways. However, neither are new. They were first used in e-mail messages and newsgroup postings many moons ago.

Here are some:

`:)   GR8 FANX 4 UR ELP C U L8R`

"Happy face: Great, thanks for your help. See you later."

ASAP	as soon as possible (been around for a long time)
ATB	all the best
BRB	be right back
BBFN	bye for now
BYKT	but you knew that
4EVRYRS	for ever yours
EOL	end of lecture
H8	hate
HAND	have a nice day
HTH	hope this helps
H&K or XOXOX	hugs and kisses
IMHO	in my humble opinion
JK	just kidding
KIT	keep in touch
L8	later
RUOK	Are you OK?
TX	thanks

4: E-mail

Emoticons (viewed sideways)			
:O	yelling	>:(	very angry
[!]	hug	;)	winking
:Y	a quiet aside	:-/	undecided
oo-	puzzled	:-\	sceptical
:)	happy	;-))	very happy
:(	sad	;-((	very sad
:t	pouting	:-7	wry smile

FIVE:

Newsgroups

Essentially, the Internet is a means of finding information and communicating with others. We looked at e-mail and instant messaging in the last Chapter as a means of communication. Another source for both information and communication is *newsgroups.* It will never replace e-mail for quick communication but it is definitely a valuable online source when you are looking for specific information or help with a problem. Unlike web sites, newsgroups have no images or sound, it is pure text based, more like a public e-mail service.

Newsgroups originated in North Carolina in 1979. It was originally called USENET, and still is, though *newsgroups* has become more common.

A newsgroup is a continuous public discussion about a particular topic. You can join a newsgroup at any time and become part of a huge conversation between hundreds or even thousands of people. Some simply like to eavesdrop on what others are talking about, known as *lurkers.*

What is Usenet?

Here is an excerpt from:

`http://www.faqs.org/faqs/usenet/what-is/part1/`

> *Usenet is a world-wide distributed discussion system. It consists of a set of "newsgroups" with names that are classified hierarchically by subject. "Articles" or "messages" are "posted" to these newsgroups by people on computers with the*

appropriate software -- these articles are then broadcast to other interconnected computer systems via a wide variety of networks.

So, let us see what all this is about.

When I send an e-mail message, it is directed at one particular person or group of people. With a newsgroup message (called a *posting* or *article*), it is aimed at anyone who happens to chance upon it. It is an electronic way of putting up a message on a public noticeboard. Anyone who passes by may read it and respond to it. The messages, like e-mail, are pure text.

As an example, I had a problem with HTML which I could not solve. One Thursday afternoon, I decided to post my problem on the noticeboard of the newsgroup which discusses HTML problems. The group name is:

`comp.infosystems.www.authoring.html`

which we can talk about later. The next morning, I had a spare minute or two, so I decided to see whether anyone had replied. To my delight, two people had responded both with correct solutions, one from the States and one from France.

How Newsgroups work

Once you have posted your message to a particular newsgroup (there are over 40,000!), it is stored on a news server. Most browsers support newsgroups and contain a newsgroup program officially known as a *newsreader*. This program sends your messages automatically to the one news server to which it is connected. Most large organisations and ISPs have connections to a news server.

A news server is different to a web server, which stores web pages created by one organisation. Anyone requesting one of the web pages can only do so by going to that unique organisation's web server using the `http` protocol. News servers use the Network News Transfer Protocol (`nntp`). There are hundreds, if not thousands of news servers scattered world-wide. Each is in communication with one or more.

When my news server was forwarded my message, it was stored just on that one server. Every so often, one server will contact another with all the new messages it has received. This other server will compare its own messages for the given newsgroups with those it has just received. By comparing the messages, it can extract the new messages and store them locally. In turn, this news server will contact another server and the process is repeated. In time all newservers will be updated with all the new postings. Thus, someone contacting their local news server will eventually receive my new article.

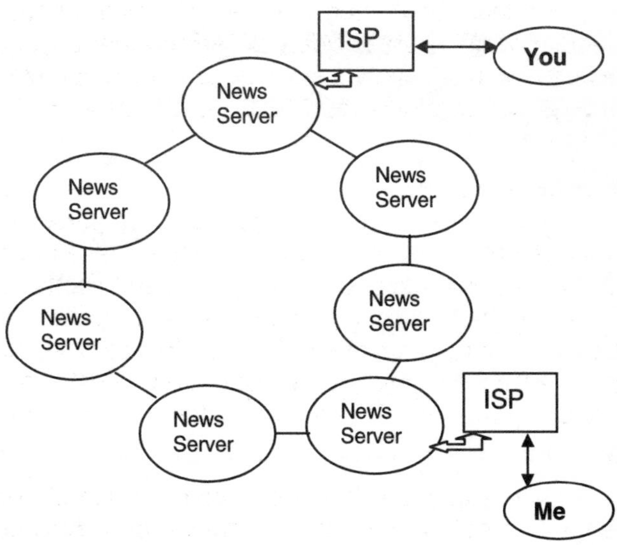

When someone replies, my local news server will eventually receive and update its messages so that I will be able to read the response. The whole process of updating is continuous.

How to find a Newsgroup

Clearly, with so many thousands of newsgroups in existence, there is a problem finding the name of the newsgroup you want. Usenet (`www.usenet.org`) has a great deal of information but you need to know your way around. So try something simple. I happen to be smitten by Errol Garner (jazz pianist). If I wanted to discuss his techniques, I would need to know the newsgroup category he would belong to.

There are several very good web sites which help out. The following illustrates the Google site, where you can search by subject, any subject: `http://groups.google.com/`

I simply typed in 'Errol Garner'

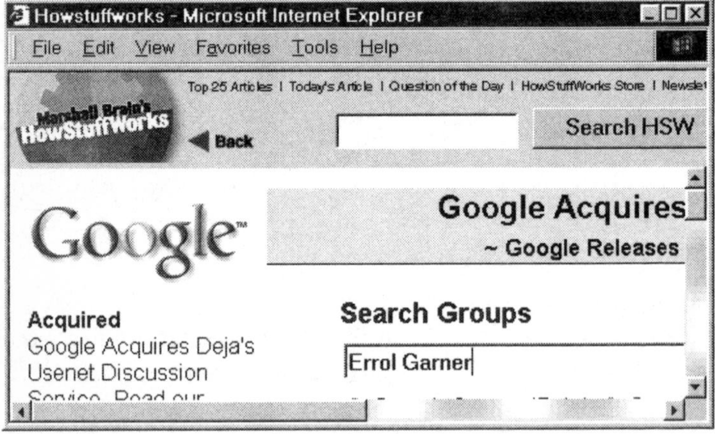

In 12 seconds, it came back with the newsgroup address: `rec.music.makers.piano` along with specific postings related to the great man.

I made a note of the group, called up my newsreader program from within my browser, found the Newsgroup *subscribe to* button and clicked. I entered the newsgroup name, clicked on the subscribe button again, and that was it. I had now subscribed to the group and could begin asking my own questions or simply read what others had posted. Of course, it was not devoted solely to Errol Garner, but at least I was in the group which would be willing to exchange thoughts.

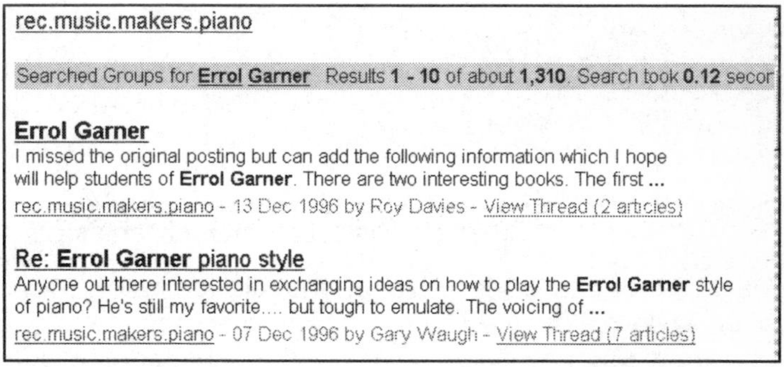

rec.music.makers.piano

Searched Groups for **Errol Garner** Results **1 - 10** of about **1,310**. Search took **0.12** secor

Errol Garner
I missed the original posting but can add the following information which I hope will help students of **Errol Garner**. There are two interesting books. The first ...
rec.music.makers.piano - 13 Dec 1996 by Roy Davies - View Thread (2 articles)

Re: **Errol Garner** piano style
Anyone out there interested in exchanging ideas on how to play the **Errol Garner** style of piano? He's still my favorite.... but tough to emulate. The voicing of ...
rec.music.makers.piano - 07 Dec 1996 by Gary Waugh - View Thread (7 articles)

It is usually quite simple to subscribe to newsgroups, but each browser will have slightly different buttons and store them in different menus.

Newsgroup Names

Groups are identified by a hierarchical set of categories. There were originally eight main top level categories, such as:

- comp (computers)
- humanities (arts and culture)
- rec (recreational)

- sci (science)
- uk (United Kingdom only groups, 385 groups - jobs, sport, adverts, etc.)

and so on. Try www.usenet.org.uk for a complete list of all UK newsgroups.

These top levels were further subdivided, using a full-stop to separate one level from another. Humanities has eight subgroups, rec has 725, etc. Some of these have other sub-levels. For example, rec.music has a further 102, one being *makers* which has more sub-divisions (well I stopped counting). Many of the group names are self explanatory such as:

uk.jobs.offered
uk.local.geordie
talk.environment
uk.sport.football.clubs
rec.arts.tv.uk.eastenders (or coronation-st)
sci.med.prostate.cancer (offering advice, news, research. It is not all fun and games.)

Because of the sheer size of the groups, most news servers do not carry every available newsgroup. If the one you want is not available, you would need to contact your news server administrator and see whether it can be added.

News servers are owned by ISPs or organisations with their own computer networks such as schools, universities and companies.

Chat Rooms

Certain companies such as AOL and TalkCity.com provide what are called *chat rooms*. It is similar to a private e-mail group where a group of people can 'converse'. Usually, one has to sign up with the company and then select one of the rooms to visit, for example the music, sport, teens, family, people, health room, and so on. Anyone else in the room, can see any of the messages typed in.

Chat rooms are most effective when you want to get an immediate response, communicate with more than one person, meet new people, receive or impart some information.

Some ISPs are now becoming more responsible and are monitoring what goes on in their chat rooms. Everyone is able to see what is being typed.

For those concerned about the dangers of chat room for children, see pages 114 and 121.

5: Newsgroups

SIX:

Searching for Information

We now look at the ways in which we can *find* information on the WWW. The previous two chapters discussed the ways by which the Internet can be used to communicate with others. The Internet also provides a means of locating information stored in one of the millions of web sites scattered throughout the world.

Three ways of finding Information

1. You know the address, the so-called URL (see page 9), the term given to an Internet address. These are very familiar to most people:

`http://www.bbc.co.uk`

You simply type it into the address location box of your browser and wait for the page to be displayed. If you do not specify a particular page after the site address, each web server has a *home page* which it will send to your browser.

2. You are reading a web page and find a link to another page. You click on the link and that link page will be displayed.

3. When neither of the above is available, you need to use one of the many search tools. This is what we discuss in this chapter. In case you are wondering, finding information via search tools has become an art. Full-time researchers specialise in being able to delve deeply into the Internet by using advanced search techniques and the right sort of search tool. We can all become 'expert' in this skill, but only after some practice.

Using Search Engines

If an organisation's web page is on a server which is connected to the Internet, then anyone can visit and read that page and make a mental or written note about its contents. If this page has links to other pages, then those links can be followed and their contents 'memorised'.

There are many companies which make a living out of doing precisely that. They have a list of sites and visit all of them on a regular basis to see what they have to offer, what is new and what has been changed since their last visit.

Details of what is found and where it was found is kept in a huge *index* or database. These indexes are owned and maintained by the individual search companies. When someone uses their search engine to find information, the keywords are matched against their own index and a list of web pages and their addresses is returned to the user.

How do they get the Lists?

Search engines are owned by organisations which have procured a list of major and minor site addresses and they regularly visit each of the sites on their list. These lists can be obtained in many ways. InterNIC (Internet Network

Information Center) is an organisation which handles Internet domain name registration (see page 69). Each new site has to register its site address for approval. In the UK, this can be done through various companies. These lists can be obtained by other organisations.

Many Web masters 'announce' their sites to the major search tools in the hope that these search providers will visit their sites and include their pages in their database. In other words, lists of sites can be obtained from a variety of sources, just like ordinary mailing lists.

How do they create the Indexed Database?

There are basically two methods by which the search companies collect the information held in their databases. One method is to send out *computer programs* to do all the hard work of visiting sites and returning with what they have found. These programs are the true search engines and are frequently referred to as *crawlers* or *spiders* or *robots* or just *bots*. AltaVista, Excite and Northern Light are three such excellent examples.

The other method uses *people*. They use their browsers, just as we do. They visit site addresses, look at the home pages and list all the material they find. They will also follow links to other pages mentioned. The proper term for this method is a *directory listing* or simply *directory*. Yahoo! and LookSmart are two examples.

Search Tools

I use the term *tools* because there are five of them. Typically, *search engines* is the term most of us use, but in practice this is but one of the five.

There are five main categories of search tools:

- search engines
- directories, also called *hierarchies* or *subject trees*

- meta-search engines
- Web guides or channels for general topics, e.g.:
  entertainment, cars, travel, people, businesses, Usenet groups, health, finance, news items, etc.
- specialised search tools for specific topics, e.g.:
  StreetMap - for street maps of the UK
  Northern Light - has a series of special collections related to various main subjects such as medicine, law, news

Search Engines

A true search engine is a computer program which visits a web site and looks at the home page. It follows links from the home page to other pages. This implies that if other web pages are not mentioned on a home page, then they may not be found. Some search engines sample a web site and will stop following links after a certain level. Others dutifully follow each link regardless of the depth it might lie down.

Some make a list of each word, whereas others will select certain words based on some pre-determined algorithm. The search engine returns all the links and keywords it has found and these are stored in a huge *index*. Search keywords entered by users are then matched against this index.

When we visit a web site via our browser, we are in fact behaving like a search engine. We do it manually, whereas search engines are programs designed to visit sites automatically and return lists of what they have found.

Directories

In some cases, human editors, employed by directory providers, visit sites and compile a short description of whatever they think is of value.

The material is collated and compiled into categories and sub-categories. For example, there may be a *travel* category and another on *blood pressure* and the categories could be sub-divided as follows:

Main category	Sub-categories
Travel:	UK
Europe	Italy France, etc.
....	....
USA	New York Disney World Grand canyon, etc.
Blood Pressure:	cardiology heart disease hypertension heart (physiology), etc.

Some people refer to these directories as *hierarchies* or *search trees* because of the structure of the index. Here is an example from Yahoo! for *blood pressure*:

Yahoo! Site Matches (1 - 18 of 62) Show by relevance | Grouped by category

Sites categorized in Yahoo! that match your search.

Health > Diseases and Conditions > Hypertension

- High **Blood Pressure** - information from the American Heart Association.
- How to Keep Your **Blood Pressure** Under Control
- Hypertension Network, Inc. - HTN links patients and physicians with a common interest in high **blood pressure**.

When a search phrase is entered by users, this is matched against the categories in their index and a list of sites and web pages is returned to the user.

There are also *hybrid search engines*. These are pure search engines which also have an associated directory, so that you get the best of both worlds.

Meta search engines

Meta search engines use both methods from a variety of different search engines and directories. Today, many search tools are meta search engines.

For those really into research, these multi and meta search engines are very important. There are many of them and the one you choose depends on your personal preference. Their names will not be familiar, except to the experts, so try the excellent site below for a comparison of such search tools. Here are two taken from SearchIQ at:

`www.zdnet.com/searchiq/directory/multi.html`

The IQ is a rating, where IQ 100 is average.

> Queryserver *IQ 140*
> *A set of meta search engines that provides user options to customize results and groups findings by topic. Includes meta search options for general searches, financial searches, health/ medical, news, and government searches.*
> *Using the general use metasearch engine with its clean layout, we found this metasearch engine easy to use, providing highly relevant listings from the ten search engines it covers and it organizes the findings into logical groupings. Some redundant listings included, yet overall one of most useful metasearch tools currently available. Worth a try!*
>
> Vivisimo IQ 140
> *One of a new generation of metasearch engines. Like a handful of other metasearch engines, Vivisimo provides comprehensive coverage,*

finding relevant listings. In addition Vivisimo clusters like listings. You can scroll through these on the main part of the page or click on the handy folders on the left hand side of the page. Either way this additional organization makes it easier to navigate the search results and find what you are looking for more quickly. A lean and simple design along with options for configuring the page view (only in Internet Explorer) make this new tool among the top ten search tools we've reviewed."

Web guides

Web guides are major sites, sometimes called *portals*, such as the Netscape, MSN, Ask Jeeves, which provide a list of topics you can look up, such as finance, sport, games, travel, etc. The Netscape version is shown below.

The illustration below shows several of the tools, search engines, directories and a web guide. It is taken from Netscape's *Search* button.

Specialised search sites

Specialised search sites concentrate on one or more particular topics.

Streetmap.uk clearly concentrates on providing maps of most parts of the UK.

`http://www.streetmap.co.uk/`

Webshots has many images and pictures which you can download for free.

`http://www.webshots.com/homepage.html`

Ask Jeeves, apart from being a meta search engine, will also provide dictionary definitions of topics you search for: `http://www.askjeeves.com/` or try the following if you wish to restrict your searches to its UK site: `http://www.ask.co.uk/`

Some examples

There are many search tools running into hundreds, here are some of my favourites, mainly because they work for me. If I am not sure where to look, I frequently try *Ask Jeeves*. It will list any of its own findings along with some interesting related questions as shown in Figure 6.1.

You asked: dinosaurs

Please help me clarify your question by selecting from the list below:

Where can I find out about the Jim Henson series Dinosaurs ?

Which dinosaur had the largest skull ?

What can you tell me about the type of dinosaurs called Abelisaurs ?

When it comes to dinosaurs, are all fossil animals dinosaurs ?

Where can I read a fact file about the dinosaur called Albertosaurus ?

Figure 6.1: Ask Jeeves showing related questions

I have also found answers from the US to the following questions:

- Where can I find facts about the dinosaur species Acanthopholis ?
- Where can I learn about dinosaur digs ?
- Where can I read about the two new dinosaurs found in New Mexico?

People with similar questions have found these sites useful:

- KT.html
  What were the dinosaurs, and how did they live? Join the Dinosaur Society
- Dinosaurs and the Expanding Earth - Contents
  Comment Archives (before December 1998) Comment Archives (Dec 1998-July 2000) The current number of visitors is: Dinosaurs and the Expanding Earth One explanation for the gigantic scale of pre-historic life Contents Front page The following is a full...

Figure: 6.2 Other related Web pages

It will provide a list of sites from its own sources as well as a list pages taken from other sources to which it has links. In this way, I am sometimes able to home in on one particular search engine. These are shown in Figures 6.2 and 6.3.

Figure 6.3: Results from other search Engines shown by Ask Jeeves

6: Search Tools

Here are two more worthy tools, the first is a search engine with specialised collections, the other a directory.

> *"**Northern Light** is another favorite search engine among researchers. It features a large index of the web, along with the ability to cluster documents by topic. Northern Light also has a set of "special collection" documents that are not readily accessible to search engine spiders. There are documents from thousands of sources, including newswires, magazines and databases. Searching these documents is free, but there is a charge of up to $4 to view them. There is no charge to view documents on the public web -- only for those within the special collection. Northern Light opened to general use in August 1997.*
>
> ***Yahoo** is the web's most popular search service and has a well-deserved reputation for helping people find information easily. The secret to Yahoo's success is human beings. It is the largest human-compiled guide to the web, employing about 150 editors in an effort to categorize the web. Yahoo has well over 1 million sites listed. Yahoo also supplements its results with those from Google (beginning in July 2000, when Google takes over from Inktomi). If a search fails to find a match within Yahoo's own listings, then matches from Google are displayed. Google matches also appear after all Yahoo matches have first been shown. Yahoo is the oldest major web site directory, having launched in late 1994. "*

The above is taken from another excellent web site, Search Engine Watch, which is part of `internet.com`, hence the American spelling:

"*Search Engine Watch provides tips and information about searching the web, analysis of the search engine industry and help to site owners trying to improve their ability to be found in search engines. The site was created by Danny Sullivan an Internet consultant and journalist who continues to maintain the site for internet.com. He is assisted by associate editor Chris Sherman.* "

Here is the useful web site address where details of their free monthly newsletters are available. (A must for anyone who is serious about searching the WWW.)

`http://searchenginewatch.com/`

Do you Surf or Crawl?

People *surf* the Net looking for information, whereas search engines are said to *crawl* the Net.

It is said, but difficult to prove, that search tools have only crawled one-third of the Web sites.

6: Search Tools

SEVEN:

Where the Internet Came From

The Internet allows one person via their own computer to contact someone else's computer anywhere in the world. The two people do not have to have the same type of computer and probably will not. They could have an IBM PC, a Mac, a Unix workstation[1] or a large mainframe. The Internet is an international network comprising many different types of computers. To make contact, each person requires:

- a computer which is linked to an ISP network (via a modem in their own home or by a direct line from their office)
- software which can send information over the Internet as well as receive information and display it on a screen, such as an e-mail program or web browser

Networks have existed for several decades, so what made the Internet so special? Simply, it is difficult to ***destroy***. This makes more sense once we understand how networks operate. We shall, then, be in a position to appreciate the Internet itself.

What is a network?

The original concept of a network came about for several reasons, one being that a person at one computer wanted

---

[1] These are larger and more powerful than PCs or Macs and are often used to control the transmission of electronic mail messages between our smaller computers.

to send information to someone else at another computer or use some scarce resource such as an expensive printer. To do so, both computers had to be connected together, i.e. networked. Let us assume a building with ten micro computers scattered around in various offices. If they could be linked together, then they could send messages to each other rather than having to rely on their internal mail system.

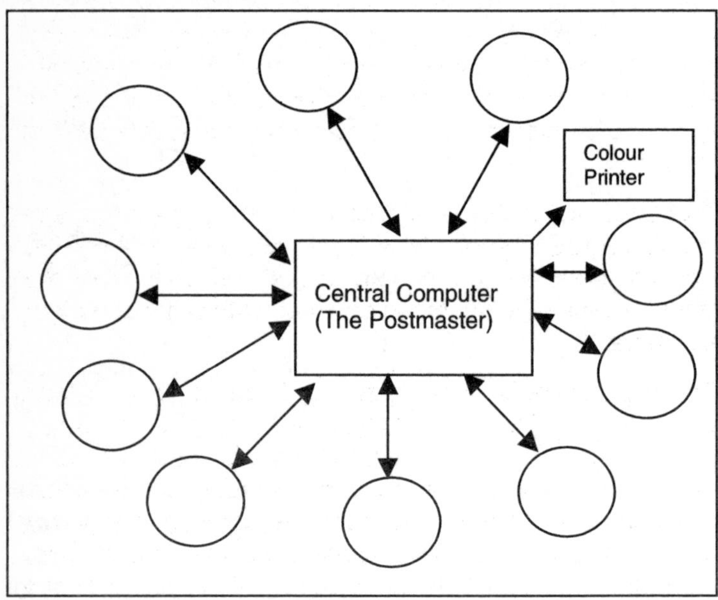

Figure 7.1: Simple network

For one machine to send a message to another machine, something has to organise and control the whole operation. (See Figure 7.1.) This is an eleventh computer complete with specially written programs which can receive messages from any one of the ten machines and redirect them to the correct person (machine). This is what the postmaster does at a local post office, indeed, this special computer is frequently referred to as a *postmaster*. It is more efficient to have one machine dedicated to this task rather than all ten linked to each other.

If I wish to send a message to Ms X, I would use the software on my machine, say an electronic mail (e-mail) program, to compose (type) the message and to send it to the postmaster. When Ms X switches on her machine, she would use her e-mail program (which could be different to mine) to contact the postmaster to check whether she has any mail. The postmaster would forward the mail and Ms X's e-mail program would display my message on her screen.

Now the point is this. If I wanted to destroy the entire set-up, all I would need to do is to destroy one machine, the eleventh one, the postmaster, the central one. Then the other ten would be unable to communicate with each other any more.

Communication is important, not least to the military, particularly in time of war. They need to keep in contact through one of many different means and one such method is via a computer network. However, if the central postmaster is destroyed, so is the entire network. It was the American military who devised the Internet concept, originally called ARPAnet, whereby there is no *one* centralised system but *many*. If one of these is destroyed, the remainder can still function. (See Figure 7.2. Put your finger over any one of the centres and you will see that the others can still function.)

Networks were developed not only to send e-mail but also to share scarce resources such as high quality printers, scanners, as well as data bases and programs.

7: The Internet

Four basic categories of networks grew up: local area networks (LANs) for use in a restricted area such as a building; wide area networks (WANs) linking computers scattered over a town, country or continents; bulletin board systems (BBS - later to become USENET) whereby people 'posted' information for others to read; and, the Internet.

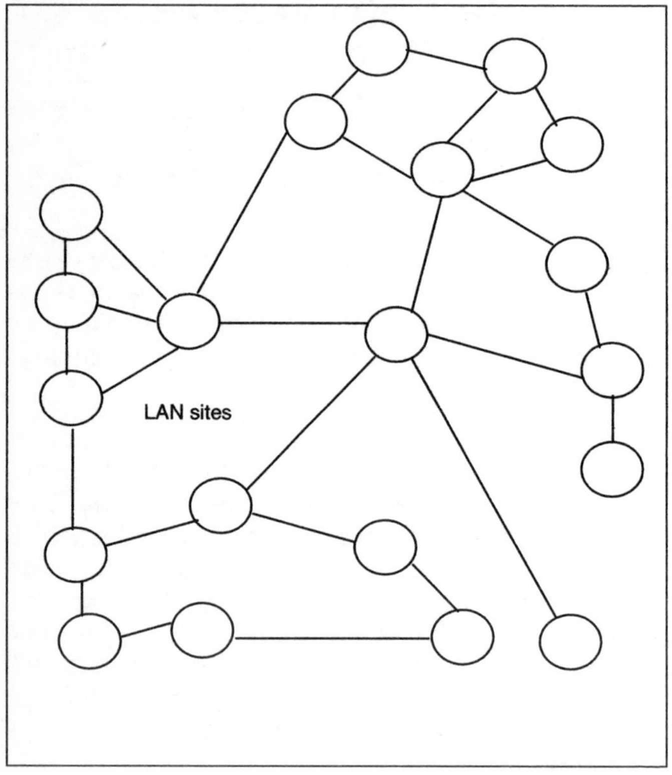

Figure 7.2: Interconnecting LANs to form a WAN

The ARPAnet

The Internet was conceived in 1969 by the American Defence Department when the Cold War and the Vietnam War were causing civil unrest. It was an experiment in how to design a network which could still function even if one part were to be destroyed by, say, a bomb attack, terrorist activity, an earthquake or simply someone cutting through a cable. It was called the ARPAnet.[2]

A working model was created and academics and researchers were also allowed access. They soon became addicted. Elsewhere in the States, Scandinavia and the UK, demands for similar networks began to grow.

Around the same time, local area networks (LANs) were being developed. It was a gradual process until about 1983 when desktop workstations became available and, then, local networking really exploded. This was due to the advent of cheap microcomputer technology. Some of the local networks wanted to link up to the ARPAnet to access facilities previously available only to a limited number of researchers and academics.

JANET

JANET (Joint Academic Network) is a private, government funded network. All further and higher education organisations are connected to JANET as are all the research council institutions. JANET has a Connection Policy which defines who can connect to the network and an Acceptable Use Policy defining what it can be used for. It is connected to the equivalent academic networks in other countries and to many commercial networks in the UK and abroad forming part of the global internet.

---

[2] The Advanced Research Project Agency network. They had four sites in 1969, 4000 by 1983.

7: The Internet

Here is the JANET backbone. The smaller balls indicate regional networks entry points linking to the larger Core Points of Presence.

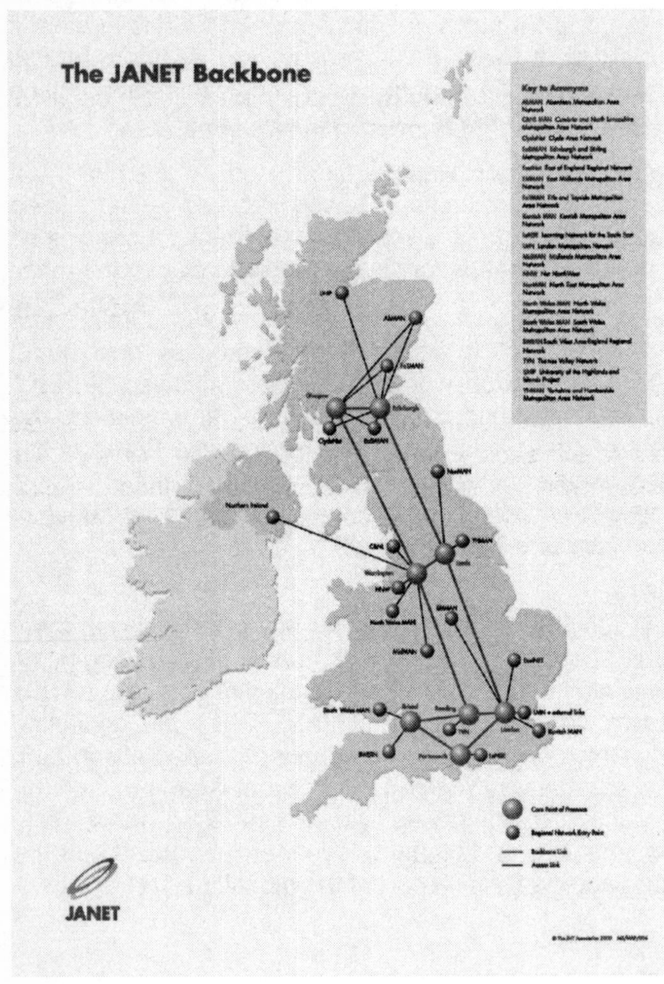

The above was taken, with permission, from JANET - the URL is: `http://www.ja.net`.

More details may be found at:

`http://www.ja.net/janet-sites/index.html`

The major routes or backbones of the Internet are unknown to most users. Backbone servers such as vBNS, Energis and NTT carry most of the information.

National Science Foundation

Private networks were also being developed during this period by companies and other organisations. One of the most important of these was the NSFNET system commissioned by the National Science Foundation, an agency of the American government.

In the late 1980s, it created supercomputer centres at renowned American universities. Because of the vast expense of each centre only five were created. The intention was to make the resources at these centres available for scholarly research elsewhere. The problem was how?

NSF approached ARPAnet to use their system. This ploy failed mainly because of bureaucratic and staffing problems. So, NSF decided to build their own network but based on the ARPAnet technology. The five sites were inter-connected by telephone lines able to transmit two A4 pages of data per second (56,000 bits[3] per second, slow by today's standards). But what about the other outlying centres, how were they to join up? Clearly direct lines from each outstation anywhere in the States to one of the five Centres would become prohibitively expensive.

---

[3] Short for **B**inary dig**IT**, 0 & 1, the system used to store information in computers.

The solution was to create regional network centres, with each one linking up to the next to form a chain. Each chain was eventually linked to one of the five main sites, collectively referred to as the *backbone*. Since each of the five sites were connected, one computer in any one of the chained links could communicate with another computer in any of the other chains as well as with any one of the five main centres.

It worked, and suddenly regional centres had access to all the data and research available anywhere in the network as well as the use of the special computing facilities at any of the five supercomputer sites. But it worked too well and became overloaded. In 1987, Merit Network Inc. was given a contract to manage and upgrade the network. Faster telephone lines and faster computers were installed and this process of upgrading has had to continue to the present day and must do so into the future.

So successful was the work resulting from the NSF project that it funded connections for other centres but only on the condition that they allowed yet others to connect to them. The Internet had arrived! Not just as a single network but as a network of networks, with more joining in every month.

It was not long before other universities, libraries and research centres in major corporations wanted to join in and not only from the US but also from abroad. Today, of course, it is not restricted to research and education. Neither is access restricted solely from the office computer. Many want to continue their work from their home computers as well as from the new Internet access devices based on mobile phones.

To illustrate the cost-effectiveness of the Internet, a colleague of mine was doing research in a particular field which demanded the use of a very powerful supercomputer. He had to connect to a university in the States which had such a computer. Some of his work had to be carried out from his home via a modem and telephone link to the States. Each dial-in session was, of course, expensive. It was a direct call to the States after all. Then the Internet arrived. By connecting to a local Internet network he had the same access to the States computer as before but at the cost of a local telephone call.

A Common Language

It was not purely the existence of many networks that brought about the Internet. Of far greater significance was how they all managed to 'talk' to each other. The reality of the Internet is a mass of different computers using a variety of operating systems which cannot communicate with (talk to) each other. For example, basic PCs, Macs, Unix workstations, IBM mainframes, Suns, etc., a real Tower of Babel. Some common tongue was required so that all these different computer systems could understand each other. This was another major achievement of the ARPAnet, perhaps the real accomplishment.

The ARPAnet system devised rules (or *protocols* as they are known) for transmitting data, the so-called *Internet Protocol* (IP). This is discussed in detail in Chapter 8.

As the growth in networks increased, so the computers attached to them became many and diverse. If these different systems wanted to communicate with each other, a common language had to be devised. One already existed and worked, the IP protocol; ergo, use that one. It was fortunate that many of the network systems decided to adopt the same IP protocol which ARPAnet had developed, mainly for purely practical reasons.

7: <u>The Internet</u>

With the desktop workstation explosion in the mid-80s many of these came with the Berkeley Unix operating system which, fortunately, had also adopted the IP networking protocol. It was this common tongue that led to the world-wide development of the Internet.

NSFNET, although denied use of the ARPAnet's communications, nevertheless based their network strategy on the IP technology. In other words, all those networks mushrooming up all over the place already had a common tongue and were able to link together with comparative ease because they could all talk the same language no matter what operating system or hardware manufacturer they used.

It is now time to get down to some technical details, to see how the Internet actually works. It is not everyone who wants to know how things work, but should you take the time, it will explain many of the strange things which appear, such as the four figure numerical addresses. It will also clarify much of the jargon, such as domain names, IP address, hosts, client-servers, hypertext. This will all help to understand what the network gurus are trying to say to you when you ask them simple questions.

EIGHT:

How the Internet Works

In order to understand how the Internet works we need to appreciate some technical terms, otherwise it will always remain 'a bit of a mystery'.

At the basic level, a wire from my computer links it to a local area network (LAN). The wire to this LAN could be a direct line or a modem connection via the telephone system or a cable connection to my ISP's LAN. My local network has other wires linking it to yet more networks which have wires to yet other networks. It is my local network which provides the link between my computer and all the other networks which collectively make up the Internet.

Most of the Internet is made up of the telephone system which links one network to another and across continents. Today, satellites, cable and wireless links are also available. However, to understand how the Internet works the telephone system is not a good analogy. The telephone system is a *circuit switched* network, which means that if you dial someone and make a connection, no one else can contact that person until you finish the conversation and no one else can contact you. Your connection is 'frozen'.

A better analogy is the postal system which is a *packet switched* network. Information is sent in envelopes and many people all over the country can drop their letters in the post box at the same time. More important, is that all of them can be forwarded to the same address and arrive on the same day. Other letters do not have to wait until one letter is sent and received before the next letter is allowed to be sent. No one person can, therefore, hog the entire network. We can all share the service and all at the same time. Let us relate this to the Internet.

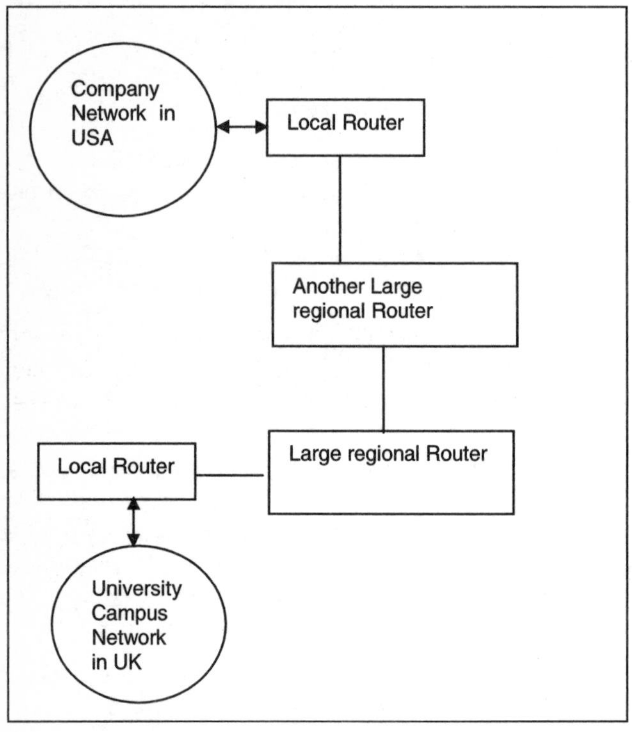

Figure 8.1: Routers - the key to the Internet

Figure 8.1 shows two networks. One is a university campus-wide network in the UK, another is a company network. Note that there are other boxes called *routers*. It is these routers which forward information from one network to another and thus connect a user at one site to another user elsewhere. Without routers each network would remain independent, alone. It is a piece of the jigsaw which we seldom hear about but it is the technology most responsible for allowing the Internet to exist at all. They form the backbone of the Internet. Some of the largest routers are made by Cisco Systems, Inc, a company specialising in networking hardware. Some can handle as many as 60 million packets a second. A *packet* is a term used for the data which is sent over the Internet. We discuss this in more detail below.

Routers, then, connect networks together. They are computers which know about other routers in their vicinity. When I send information to somewhere beyond my company's network, it is forwarded to my local router. This one decides which of the routers it knows about is the best one to forward my data to so that it can more quickly arrive at its destination. In order for the router to make such a decision, it looks at the address of the machine to which I wish to send my information.

This is what our local postmaster does. When I wish to send a letter to someone, I follow the Post Office's rules for creating an address: person's name, house number, road, town, county, post code, country. Likewise, over the Internet, there is a set of rules (*a protocol*) for creating network addresses. This is called the Internet Protocol (IP), first laid down by the designers of ARPAnet.

Each computer on the Internet has a unique IP address. It is by these addresses that they are identified by their own local network. Basically, it is similar to your own home address which you freely give to people so that they can contact you when necessary.

Internet Addresses

Internet addresses comprise four numbers, separated by full stops and each one less than 256, e.g. `122.234.34.8`. (In practice we use names rather than numbers, but more of that later.) These numerical addresses, sometimes called the *dotted-quad*, go at the start of your information. The leftmost part tells the router which network you are part of, the right section tells the router which computer in that network should receive the information.

Obviously, the router needs programs to allow it to decipher addresses. This is what is known as the IP software and it sits on top of the basic wires, rather like one onion ring sits on top of another. See Figure 8.2.

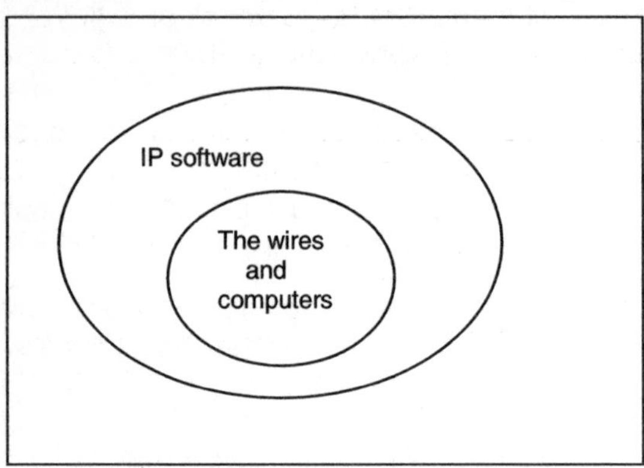

Fig: 8.2 Adding the IP Software layer

For technical reasons beyond the scope of this book, the data sent over IP networks is limited to 1500 characters. Naturally, many people want to send or receive much more than 1500 characters, little more than about 20 lines of text. This is handled by the TCP, Transmission Control

Protocol, yet another outer layer of the network onion, see Figure 8.3. It is this layer which prevents the system being monopolised by a handful of users.

Transmission Control Protocol (TCP)

TCP is so closely related to the Internet Protocol that you may often hear people refer to the TCP/IP. Suppose you have a ten page document to send to someone. You will type the document and attach it to, say, an e-mail message. It is sent off via the network. However the IP cannot handle it, it is too large. The TCP, however, can and it will rip this document into shreds (called *packets*), each of 1500 characters. It will number each one and put on the IP address of the sender and the IP address of the recipient. Each packet is passed to the IP software which is then capable of handling each packet of 1500 characters or so, and pass it on to the most convenient router.

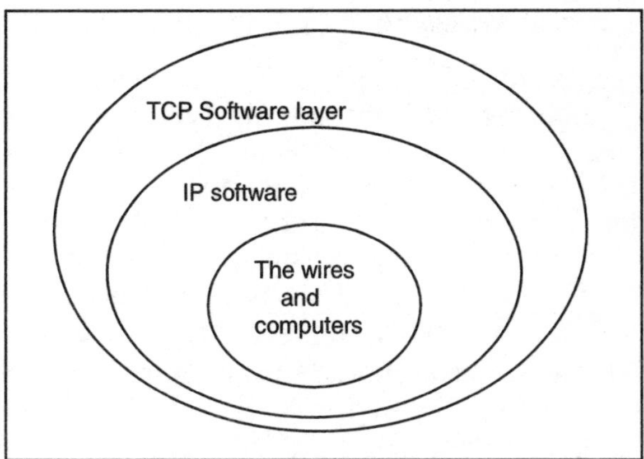

Fig: 8.3 Adding the TCP layer

When all the packets eventually arrive at the other end and possibly out of order, that network's TCP program will begin to put them together as a single document and in the right order based on the sequence numbers put on by the original TCP software.

My packets of data/information are mixed up with everyone else's packets, just like letters being placed in a post-bag. It is through the IP address and the TCP sequence number that the TCP software at the local network collates all the individual packets and assembles them into single units.

To users, exactly what the TCP does is effectively invisible (*seamless* is the jargon term). I send a message, a three page document to Ms Y. She sees a three page document on her computer screen. The fact that during transmission it was ripped into little bits (packets) and re-assembled by the receiving TCP program at the other end, is something we are not normally aware of.

Suppose one of the packets gets lost during transmission, which is not unusual? Fortunately, there are various techniques used in computing to quickly detect transmission errors. When this happens, the receiving computer discards everything that has been sent and requests another complete transmission from the sending machine[1]. Eventually, one of the re-transmissions will be correct. Both ends need to keep in contact until the receiving end is satisfied that everything has been received. This is a vast improvement on the manual postal system in which when a letter gets lost, it frequently stays lost.

---

[1] This proves to be more reliable than the postal service which cannot request another 'transmission' of your letter.

Incidentally, each packet of data need not necessarily be forwarded by the same set of routers. Figure 8.1 gives a very simple picture. One router is frequently in touch with several other routers. If one of these is busy, another one could be passed the next packet and may arrive ahead of the first one. Page 58 showing the JANET connection, gives a better idea.

Domain Names

If you know the numerical IP address, there is no reason why you cannot use it. Indeed, it is not uncommon to see web addresses such as:

`http://123,34,56.12/index.html`

However, life would be more simple if we could use names rather than the IP numerical system for Internet addresses. So, a long time ago, the domain name system was employed using addresses we are more familiar with, such as `www.bbc.co.uk`, `www.microsoft.com`, or the e-mail address `radio4@bbc.co.uk`.

Domain levels

Here are some typical domain names:

`www.yahoo.com` (profit making company)
`www.bbc.co.uk` (a company in the UK)
`www.ic.ac.uk` (an academic organisation in the UK)
`www.mit.edu` (Massachusetts Institute of Technology, an educational institution)
`searchenginewatch.com` (one without the www, its use is only a convention)

The right hand part is the top level domain. `.com`, `.org` (non-profit making organisation), `.gov` (government), etc., as well as the 244 country specific names, such as `.fr` (France), `.cn` (China), `.nz` (New Zealand). The United

States is the only country that does not require a country domain. After all, they did invent the whole thing.

What appears to the left of that depends on how the name was created. It could simply be a institution's name, or another level down such as `.co` (for company), `.ac` (for an academic institution). These are called second level domain. There can be many more levels down. For example: `ic.ac.uk`, has three levels - `uk` being the top level, `ac` being the second and `ic` (Imperial College) being the third.

Converting Domain names into IP Addresses

When you type a domain name into your browser, requesting a web page, the browser needs to convert it into an IP numerical format. It does so by contacting its local domain name server. (We are beginning to realise that there are many types of servers on the Internet, each performing specialised tasks and interacting with each other.) When your machine was first set up for Internet access, one of the things your machine had to be told was what name server to use for converting domain names into IP addresses. Let us suppose that you want to contact the `www.howstuffworks.com` site for more information about how domain names work.

The name server may already have contacted this site earlier on in the day, in which case it may have cached (stored) the IP address. Some name servers may permanently store some of the more common site addresses, to speed up the process. But, let us suppose that yours is the first request.

At the heart of the domain name system are 13 special computers, called *root servers*, distributed around the world. All 13 contain the same vital information – this is to spread the workload and back each other up. They contain a database with all the IP addresses of the top level domain names – both the global registries such as `.com`, `.org`, etc., and the 244 country-specific registries such as `.at` (Austria), `.de` (Germany), `.pt` (Portugal).

They feed thousands of other servers scattered across the Internet – called 'Domain Name Resolvers' or just plain 'resolvers'. These servers routinely download and copy the information contained in the root servers. They are located strategically with Internet Service Providers (ISPs) or institutional networks.

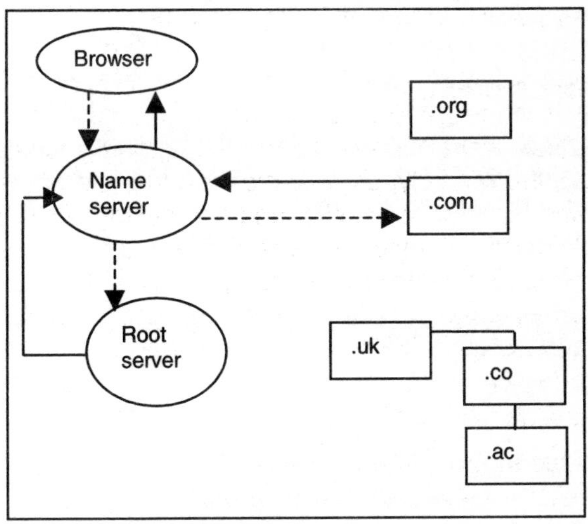

Figure 8.4: ***Dashed lines* are requests**
***Solid lines* are returned information**

When your browser is given `www.howstuffworks.com`, the browser forwards the whole address to its local name server. This notes the `.com` and because it knows the address of the server holding all the `.com` addresses (as opposed to `.org`, or `.uk`) it forwards the address to the `.com` registry server. This has a list of all the networks in the `.com` registry. It will look up the numerical IP address for `howstuffworks`. This is returned to your browser which can now forward your request to the `howstuffworks` local network. That network will send a copy of its home page back to your browser so that it can display the page.

For more detailed information, try:

`http://www.howstuffworks.com/dns.htm`

current at the time of writing.

New Net Domain names

Originally, there were 8 top level domain names, such as com, org, etc. Today, many new ones are becoming fashionable. Here are some that you may begin to see. They are self explanatory.

.arts	.golf
.auction	.school
.church	.scifi
.family	.shop

The Day the Internet Went Down

Just to illustrate the importance of domain name servers, the above heading formed the headlines of many newspapers a year or so back. The Internet would not work. The reason was that one of the main links from the UK to the rest of the world, somehow managed to get a corrupted copy of the main country domain names. Links within the UK, especially those served by JANET, were all right. But anyone trying to access non-UK sites was unable to do so.

Ways of Connecting to the Internet

Not so long ago, the only way to connect to the Internet was through our office PC which was connected to the company's LAN. From home, we would need a modem connected to our PC and access the Internet through an ISP. Both used the telephone system.

The speed at which data can travel to your PC depends on the device it is connected to. At home, a standard modem has a capacity of 56K (56 kilo bits per second). That is far too slow when downloading videos and music.

Your office may well have a T1 line which can carry data at a rate of 1.544 megabits per second, approximately 60 times more data than a normal residential modem. It is also extremely reliable -- much more reliable than an modem. Depending on what they are doing, a T1 line can generally handle quite a few people. For general browsing, hundreds of users are easily able to share a T1 line comfortably. If they are all downloading music or video files simultaneously, it would create a problem, but that is not common.

A large company needs something more than a T1 line. The following table shows some of the common line designations:

(from `www.howstuffworks.com/question372.htm`)

- DS0 - 64 kilobits per second
- ISDN - two DS0 lines plus signalling (16 kilobits per second), or 144 kilobits per second
- T1 - 1.544 megabits per second (24 DS0 lines)
- T3 - 43.232 megabits per second (28 T1s)
- OC3 - 155 megabits per second (100 T1s)
- OC12 - 622 megabits per second (4 OC3s)
- OC48 - 2.5 gigabits per second (4 OC12s)
- OC192 - 9.6 gigabits per second (4 OC48s)

Other access methods

Today, the Internet can be accessed through a cable modem, a digital subscriber line (DSL) and soon through the air.

Cable

Many people with cable TV can now get high speed connections to the Internet from their cable provider. When a cable company offers Internet access over the cable, Internet information uses the same cables. Data sent from the Internet to an individual computer looks just like a TV channel. Cable modems compete with technologies like ADSL.

ADSL

The Asymmetric Digital Subscriber Line (ADSL) super-fast technology gives households real instant Internet access. Frustrating delays will be a thing of the past. Data will be 20-50 times faster than the standard modem. This will allow movies and individual TV programmes to be sent to homes. Voice and fax data uses only a small amount of the total capacity of the telephone line. Internet data can be sent using the rest of the telephone's capacity.

Once signed up, households will remain permanently connected to the Internet without having to log on/off. It uses existing phone lines so no new connection is required. Shoppers will be able to see videos of the things they want to buy. Downloading CD quality music will take seconds. And because the ADSL does not use the same frequency as voice calls, Internet surfers will still be able to use their phones and faxes while on the computer. Many of the major ISPs are interested in using this technology.

Companies will store movies and TV shows on a central computer which can be sent off to individual homes.

Customers can use their existing TV but an engineer will have to install a set-top box and a special telephone adaptor.

Satellite

If you live too far from a phone company office for ADSL and there is no cable TV on your street, satellite Internet access may be worth considering. It's ideal for remote rural Internet users in, say, Northern Ireland and the Scottish Highlands who want broadband access. Satellite Internet uses a satellite dish instead of telephone lines or cable systems. Cable and DSL have higher download speeds, but satellite systems are about 10 times faster than a normal modem.

Airborne Systems

Many Internet users are switching to cable or DSL to increase their bandwidth (broadband), that is the amount of traffic and consequently the speed at which Internet data can be sent. However, a new type of service is being developed which will take traffic into the air. This is essentially a high speed wireless Internet connection.

Satellite Internet access is already successful. The new airborne system is similar but faster since the source of the relay is not as high up as the satellites.

Satellites orbit at several hundreds of miles above the Earth. The airborne aircraft will circle at between 9 and 11 miles above the Earth. At this altitude, they will not be affected by weather, and will be flying well above commercial air traffic. They also have a cost advantage since they do not have to be launched into space.

The airborne Internet will be seen as an addition to satellite and ground-based networks. These airborne networks will overcome the *last-mile* barriers facing conventional Internet access options. The "last mile" refers to the fact that access to high-speed cables still depends on physical proximity, and that for this reason, not everyone who wants access can have it. Providing universal access via cable or phone lines is not feasible because of the time it takes to install the wires. An airborne network will immediately overcome the *last mile* as soon as the aircraft takes off.

These airborne systems will not be completely wireless, there will still have to have ground based connection-links. Consumers will need to install an antenna on their home or office building in order to receive signals.

There are three types at present. One, the HALO network, (Angel Technologies), should be ready by 2003. A manned aircraft, called the Proteus, will circle over specific cities. Each city will have three planes, each working an eight-hour shift with two pilots splitting the flying duties.

A second player is NASA, working with AeroVironment, which will launch an unmanned craft (Helios) capable of flying over a city for six months.

The third player is Sky Station International which uses what it calls a blimp, rather than an aircraft. The first is expected to be deployed by 2002.

So, we can see that we shall have quite a choice of how we connect to the Internet and that is apart from all the new Internet devices, such as TV set tops, home phones, talking mobiles and the like. There is also a mobile phone with a pull-out 'cloth' to view web pages. Unlike the current small and fixed size of screen which today's mobile owners have to put up with, a screen cloth can be pulled out to extend the screen size and folded up when not in use. This is likely to be extended to home TV screens. Just imagine having something like a pull-down overhead projector screen attached to your wall when you want to look at the TV not to mention the saving of space.

Intranets & Extranets

Intranets:

An intranet is a private network within an organisation. It may consist of many interlinked networks scattered throughout a country or continents. Large world wide companies may create their own intranet to pass information between their various main offices. Supermarkets and banks are other obvious examples.

They connect to each other via the Internet, but only those within the organisation have access to the shared web pages, databases, and other computing resources. Essentially, it is a private Internet whereby employees can share company information.

Extranet

An extranet is again a private Internet. But instead of restricting access to authorised employees, anyone can access information, provided they have the proper authorisation.

Companies can use an extranet to:

- exclusively share product catalogues with wholesalers or those "in the trade"
- collaborate with other companies on joint development efforts
- develop and use training programs with other companies
- provide and access services provided by one company to a group of other companies, such as an online banking application managed by one company on behalf of affiliated banks
- share news of common interest exclusively with partner companies

Already, some computer manufacturers are quoting *terabytes*. Here are some of the numbers used in computers:

Name	Abbr.	Size
Kilo	K 2^10	1,024
Mega	M 2^20	1,048,576
Giga	G 2^30	1,073,741,824
Tera	T 2^40	1,099,511,627,776
Peta	P 2^50	1,125,899,906,842,624
Exa	E 2^60	1,152,921,504,606,846,976
Zetta	Z 2^70	1,180,591,620,717,411,303,424
Yotta	Y 2^80	1,208,925,819,614,629,174,706,176

Firewalls

Essentially, a firewall is a barrier to keep destructive forces away from your network. It can be either a program or hardware device that filters information coming through the Internet into a network. If the information is unwanted, it is not allowed through to the network. For example, it can block e-mail messages which contain known viruses or prevent unwanted web sites from reading files or using other resources on the network.

Network systems programmers can customise firewalls to their organisation's requirements.

Without a firewall in place, any computer attached to a network can be accessed by anyone outside of the network who knows what to do.

NINE:

Creating Web Pages

There are three ways by which you can put information onto the Web. It is assumed that you have permission to add pages to your organisation's web server, or that you have permission to put your web pages on your ISP's web server. Many offer this as a free service provided you are not trying to sell something.

You can pay someone to create the pages for you; you can use one of the special programs which can automatically convert your typed text into the web language (HTML); or you can learn HTML and do it yourself. Dreamweaver, FrontPage and Internet Assistant are three programs which automatically convert text into the HTML web language and allow you to insert images and colourful backgrounds, even create animated images. However, those who are serious about developing web pages must learn HTML. Because it is so simple, we can introduce it here.[1] One of the reasons for the dramatic explosion of the Web was that HTML is an easy language to learn, indeed, the Science Museum in London, amongst other organisations, schools and the like, teach children between 8 years and eleven to create web pages.

What is HTML?

As we all know today, when we want to look at something on the World Wide Web (WWW), we use our browser

---

1 For those who would like to know more about HTML, try: BP404 "How to create Web pages using HTML", 2nd edition, in this Babani series, by John Shelley.

program, such as Internet Explorer, Netscape, Opera, etc. Browsers do not recognise Word documents, desk top publishing documents, spreadsheet files, or anything else. They would not know how to display such files. However, they do recognise documents which have been created in HTML. It is a language which all browsers understand. It is used by authors of Web pages to tell a browser how the content of their documents should be formatted - the size of heading, the colour of text, whether to use bold or italic, the positioning of images, background colours, etc. - in other words, how a Web document should be displayed.

HTML stands for ***H***yper***t***ext ***M***ark-up ***L***anguage. The term *mark-up* comes from the printing industry. It refers to the days when a publishing editor would 'mark-up' an author's typed text so that the printer would know which words to make bold or italic, which size of type to use, say for chapter headings or footnotes, and so on.

Web authors must do this for themselves. Not only do they type in the content of the document but also the *mark-up* telling the browser how the text should look.

The original concept of the WWW was to allow people reading one document to click on a word or phrase which was blue and underlined and, lo and behold!, that reference would show up on the screen. No need to amble down to the local library or special libraries to find a copy of the reference. The blue and underlined text is called *hypertext*, it is ordinary text but has a link buried in the HTML source code which gives the Internet address of where the browser can find that page. We shall see how easy it is to create such 'hyped-up' text.

We are familiar with word processors today. We type some text, select it and click a bold button, perhaps change the colour, size and type of the text and we *instantly* see the effect on the screen. HTML is not so sophisticated. You will not see how the text will look until it is displayed by a browser.

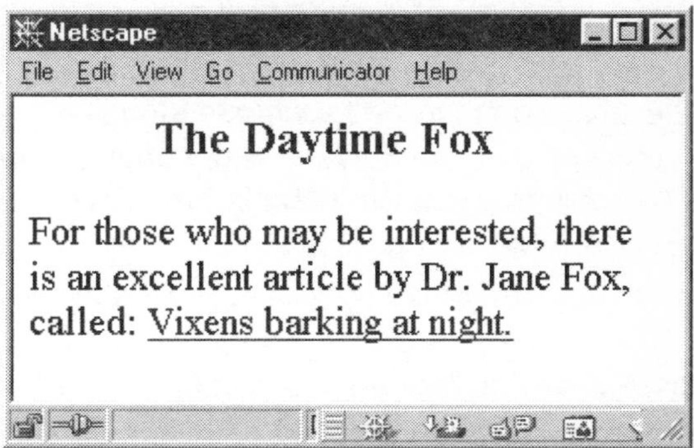

An HTML document looks more like a text formatter document which pre-dated our current word processors. With the former, the text was mixed up with all the mark-up tags. This is how we approach our web pages when writing HTML. We mix our text and mark-up tags together into what is known as the *source code* - the HTML document itself. This source code is read by a browser which will read the mark-up elements to see how the content (the text and images) is meant to be displayed. For example, here is some HTML source code:

```
Some normal text with <I> a phrase
in italic </I> and this part back
to the normal style.
```

After it has been read by the browser, it would be displayed like this in the browser's window:

Some normal text with *a phrase in italic* and this part back to the normal style.

The <I> and the </I> are the mark-up tags, sometimes called *elements*. <I> tells the browser to move into italic mode; </I> tells the browser to turn off the italic style.

Mark-up Tags

Mark-up tags are used to instruct a Web browser how to format the text. Each tag has a unique identifier enclosed in angle brackets - < >. 'B' is the tag identifier telling the browser to begin to display the text in bold. The </B> tells the browser to stop bolding. Thus:

```
Now begin to <B> bold this text. </B> Back to normal.
```

would result in a Web browser displaying:

Now begin to **bold this text.** Back to normal.

<I> is the identifier for *italic* and <U> is the identifier for underline. These and many other tags have two parts, a *start* tag and an *end* tag. The ending tag is the same as the starting tag except that it includes a forward slash - /. Everything between the pair of tags will be displayed by the browser in bold, italic or whatever, and usually in the Times New Roman typeface. (I have used Arial in this text.) For example, the following HTML source code:

```
The following words are in <B>bold</B> and in <I>italic</I> and <U>underlined</U>.
```

would be displayed by a Web browser as:

The following words are in **bold** and in *italic* and underlined.

Some tags have just one part, for example: <BR> and <HR>. The former is known as the *break* tag because it specifies that whatever text *follows* the tag must begin on the next line. <HR> causes a horizontal rule (a line) to appear across the width of the screen. These elements are called *empty tags* because they do not contain any text to be formatted, whereas, those tags which do format text are called *non-empty tags.* The latter are often referred to as *container* tags because they contain text to be formatted in some way. The *start* tag begins the desired format, the *end* tag turns off the format.

The tag name may be in uppercase, lowercase or a mixture: thus: <hR> <HR> and <hr> are all valid. However, strictly speaking, it is *not* correct to put spaces between the brackets or between the letters. Thus: < HR> or < H R > would not be recognised by some Web browsers.

A Complete HTML Document

An HTML document has two parts, a *head* and a *body.* Like human beings, a Web document should contain only *one* head and *one* body. Different browsers do different things when more than one body tag or head tag is met. Some ignore the 'error' and simply carry on, some will become confused and will not display anything which follows.

```
<HTML>
<HEAD>
<TITLE> The Home page of Fred Bloggs </TITLE>
</HEAD>
<BODY>
       Text and any images you
       want displayed....
</BODY>
</HTML>
```

The entire web page is placed within the opening <HTML> tag and the closing </HTML> tag. The Two <HEAD> tags contain a pair of <TITLE> tags which provides a title for the whole document. The <BODY> tags contain everything which you want the world to see when they visit your web page. Let us suppose that we want to display the following:

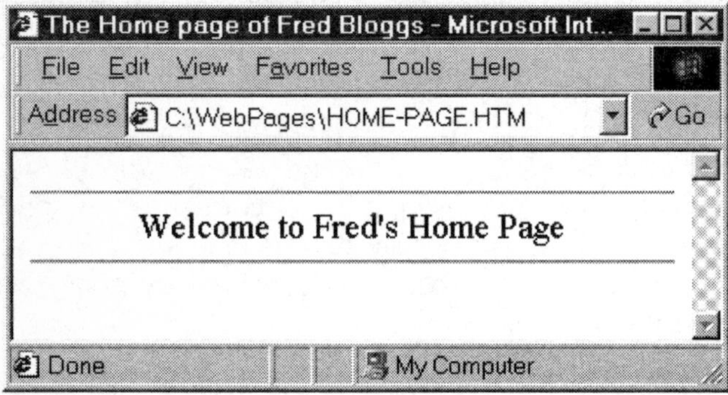

Here is the source code which creates it. Many web authors use Notepad.

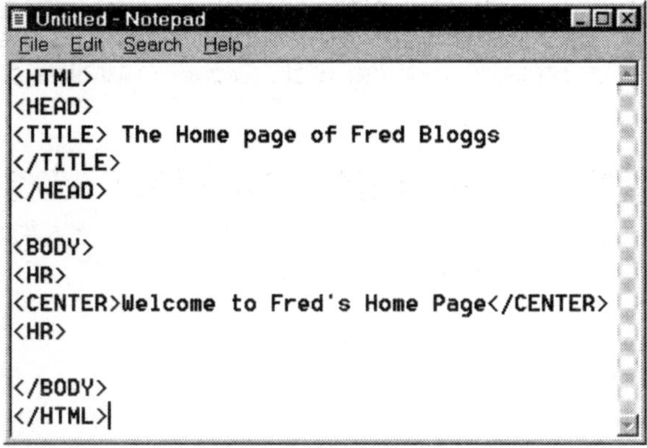

But the trick is to save it with an `htm` extension. Thus, if I have created a folder called WebPages and I want this document to be called Home-Page, I would type the following into the *Save As* dialogue box:

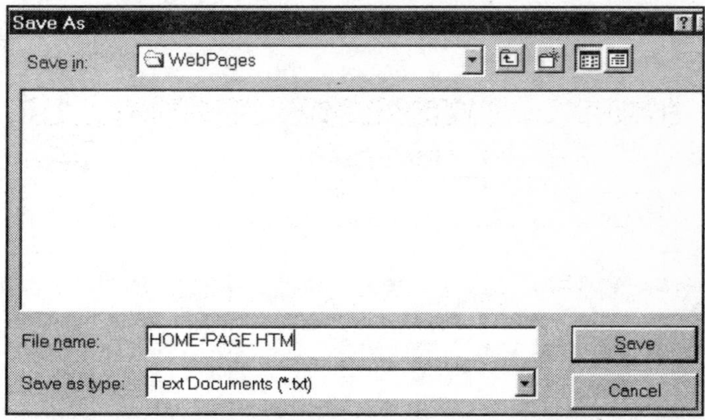

The reason that the document must be saved with an `htm` extension is to let the browser know that it is an HTML document. This file can now be opened in your browser. In Netscape or IE, this involves choosing *File*, then *Open File,* and then clicking on the OK button. You can either type the address or use the *Browse* button to locate your file.

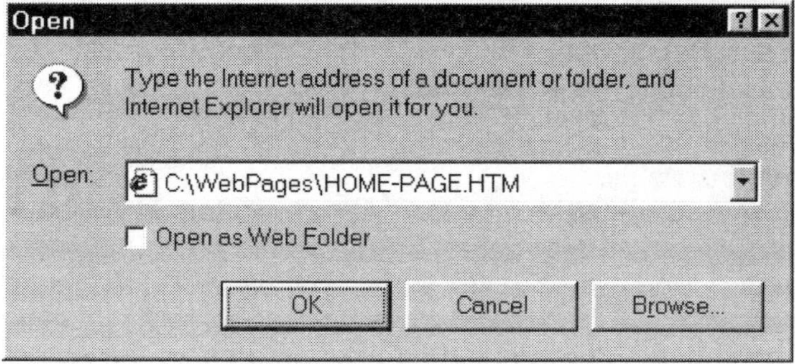

Note the use of the <CENTER> tags to centre the heading within the page. We must use the American spelling for center!

Let us now add a paragraph to tell people more about Fred. I am only going to show what goes within the <BODY> tags, but of course the rest must also be included.

```
<BODY  bgcolor="lightblue">
<HR>
<CENTER>Welcome to Fred's Home Page</CENTER>
<HR>
<P>Hi Folks. I am Fred, aged 32. I am married
with two lovely kids, Jenny aged 4 and Samuel
aged 18 months. My wife is called Rosalind
and we all live in Bootle. I am an
electrician working for myself. </P>
</BODY>
```

You can see the final web page on page 90. We have put the paragraph of text within the <P> tags (called paragraph tags). This ensures that the paragraph will stand on its own, with a line space before and after the text. Within the opening <BODY> tag we have included an extra piece of information called an attribute. It further defines what will happen. In this case we are asking for the whole web page to have a background colour (bgcolor) of light blue. Note the American spelling for color. There are three words in HTML which must be spelt in the American way: center, color and gray.

Colour Names

There are sixteen common colour names which most browsers can recognise. Those marked with an asterisk are not always accepted by some browsers. It would be safer to use their hexadecimal values. There are sixteen million colours which can be used. Apart from the above, all the rest have to be given their hexadecimal colour values. `<BODY bgcolor="#CCFFFF">`

But that is best left to a course or book on HTML.

Colour name	Hex value	Colour name	Hex value
black	"#000000"	green	"#00FF00"
silver	"#C0C0C0"	lime	"#008000"
gray (US spelling)	"#808080"	olive	"#808000"
white	"#FFFFFF"	yellow	"#FFFF00"
maroon	"#800000"	navy	"#000080"
red	"#FF0000"	blue	"#0000FF"
purple	"#800080"	teal	"#008080"
fuchsia	"#FF00FF"	aqua	"#00FFFF"
* lightblue	"#CCFFFF"	* lightgreen	"#8DF78D"
* lightyellow	"#F1EF95"	* pink	"#FF99CC"

We shall illustrate just three more features, one is to put images into a page and the second is to use the <FONT> tag to change the colour, size and typeface of text, and finally, how to link one page to another.

Adding an Image

```
<IMG SRC="splash.gif" align="right">
<P>Hi Folks. I am Fred, aged 32. I am married with two lovely kids, Jenny aged 4 and Samuel aged 18 months. My wife is called Rosalind and we all live in Bootle. I am an electrician working for myself. </P>
<IMG SRC="splash.gif" align="left">
```

Wherever the <IMG> tag is placed, that is where the image will appear on the web page. It is one of the tags which has only one part. It requires at least one attribute, the SRC (source) attribute to tell the browser the name of the image. An image is a separate file which has to be fetched by the browser and loaded into the web page when an image tag is encountered in the source code. It was saved as `splash.gif`. and stored in the same folder as the HTML file. Note the different extension used for this image. We discuss it in more detail below.

The second attribute specifies the alignment for the image - on the left or right of the page. See the final version for how it looks. The actual image was created in PhotoShop.

Changing text

```
<CENTER>
<FONT color="white" face="verdana" size="+2">
Welcome to Fred's Home Page
</FONT>
</CENTER>
```

The text within the <FONT> tags will be coloured white, using the Verdana typeface and will be twice the size of normal text. It is important to use the quotes.

Adding Hypertext Links

Finally, in this brief introduction to HTML, we shall link this page to a second page which shows Fred's interests and a photograph of his family.

This, after all, was one of the main reasons for creating the WWW, to have instant access to other pages which were referenced in a given page.

```
<BR CLEAR="all">
<P>You can see a list of
<A HREF="interests.htm">
my interests and a picture of my family
</A>
on a separate web page. </P>
Fred Bloggs <BR>
Sept. 2002 <BR>
e-mail: f.bloggs@hotmail.com
```

The text which is placed within the <A> tags will become blue and underlined when displayed by your browser. This indicates to your readers that it is hypertext. If and when this text is clicked, the browser will look at the HREF (*hypertext reference*) attribute to see what page has to be loaded.

In order to force the second paragraph to fall below the Splash image, we had to use the CLEAR="all" attribute with the <BR> tag.

Here is the complete HTML source code, followed by the page in all its glory:

```
<HTML>
<HEAD>
<TITLE> The Home page of Fred Bloggs </TITLE>
</HEAD>

<BODY  bgcolor="lightblue">
<HR>
<CENTER>
<FONT color="blue" face="verdana"
      size="+2">
Welcome to Fred's <BR> Home Page
</FONT>
</CENTER>
<HR>
<IMG SRC="splash.gif" align="right">
<P>Hi Folks. I am Fred, aged 32. I am married
with two lovely kids, Jenny aged 4 and Samuel
aged 18 months. My wife is called Rosalind
and we all live in Bootle. I am an
electrician working for myself.
<IMG SRC="splash.gif" align="left">
</P>
<BR CLEAR="all">
<P>You can see a list of
<A HREF="interests.htm"> my interests and a
```

```
picture of my family </A>
on a separate web page. </P>
<FONT SIZE="-1">
Fred Bloggs <BR>
Sept. 2002 <BR>
e-mail: f.bloggs@hotmail.com
</FONT>
</BODY>
</HTML>
```

Welcome to Fred's Home Page

Hi Folks. I am Fred, aged 32. I am married with two lovely kids, Jenny aged 4 and Samuel aged 18 months. My wife is called Rosalind and we all live in Bootle. I am an electrician working for myself.

You can see a list of my interests and a picture of my family on a separate web page.

Fred Bloggs
Sept. 2002
e-mail: f.bloggs@hotmail.com

Here is the Interest page, followed by the HTML source code:

Fred's Interests Page

I like:

Drinking
Eating junk food
Watching TV
Reading Health magazines

Return to my Home Page

```
<HTML>
<HEAD>
<TITLE> The Interests of Fred Bloggs </TITLE>
</HEAD>

<BODY  bgcolor="white">
<HR>
<CENTER>
<FONT color="blue" face="verdana" size="+2">
Fred's Interests Page
</FONT>
```

```
</CENTER>
<HR>
<IMG SRC="splash.gif" align="right">
<BR CLEAR="all">
<P>I like:
<HR>
<CENTER>Drinking<BR>
Eating junk food<BR>
Watching TV<BR>
Reading Health magazines<BR>
</CENTER>
<HR>
<IMG SRC="family.jpg" align="left">
</P>

<FONT SIZE="-1">
<A HREF="HOME-PAGE.HTM">Return to my Home
Page </A>
</FONT>
</BODY>
</HTML>
```

Notice how we included a link from the *interests* page back to the *home* page.

How many separate files were needed to complete Fred's web site? Here is the complete list, all stored in the WebPages folder.

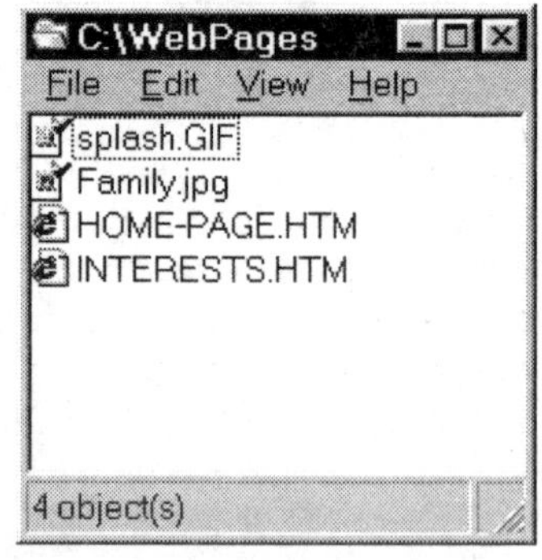

We needed one `htm` document for the home page and one for the interests page. We required two image files, one for the splash design and another for the family group. That makes four in total.

The two image files had to be created using an image processing program, PhotoShop, Image Composer, etc.

I created the circle effect and saved it as a GIF file (`splash.gif`). The family photograph would have been scanned and then saved as a JPG file (`family.jpg`). We discuss these two formats next.

Image Formats

There are many different formats for storing digital images for computer display. Each has advantages and disadvantages. At the present time, web browsers are able to recognise just a few of these formats. Thus, any image to be inserted in a document should conform to one of these formats: GIF, JPEG or PNG.

GIF

Graphics Interchange Format - with a `.gif` filename extension. It is a format which all graphical web browsers can recognise. It is especially useful if the graphical image is a logo, an icon or a banner, where there is little variation in colour detail. It can store black-and-white, greyscale and colour images, although it is limited to 256 colours per image. It is also useful when *transparent* images are required. This allows any background colour on the web page to show through the transparent areas. It also allows for *interlacing*. Usually, images are built up pixel line by pixel line starting at the top and working to the bottom. Interlacing is a technique whereby groups of lines are displayed, interspersed throughout the image, so that the entire image is seen in more and more detail giving the viewer an overall 'picture' of the image from the outset.

JPEG

Joint Photographic Experts Group is a format especially designed for storing photographic images. Its file extension is `.jpeg` or `.jpg`. It uses a 24-bit colour depth (i.e. millions of colours) and should be used when a high level of colour and detail must be preserved, for example with photographs.

Generally, speaking, JPEG format is better than GIF for photographic images. The quality is better and through its more sophisticated compression techniques the resulting files are smaller than an equivalent GIF version.
When saving an image in JPEG format, some image programs allow a *progressive* option to be chosen. It is the equivalent of the GIF interlaced format.

PNG
The last format which browser programs can recognise and display is the Portable Network Graphic (`.png`). Like GIF, it allows for transparency, interlacing and image compression. It has better colour quality than GIF so why have I given up on using `png` images? The problem is that Navigator and IE tend to show the colours differently. The same image often looks much darker in IE than in Netscape, to the extent that the detail becomes blurred. Try it out and make up your own mind.

It is hoped that you can begin to see that HTML is not a very difficult language. One has to be careful about putting in the angle brackets (< >) and to put an equals symbol after an attribute, with quote marks around the value it takes: `align="right"` for example. You need to know which tags require an opening and closing tag and which have only one. But after a short while, this becomes second nature.

TEN:

The Future of the Internet - XML

There is a new development taking place which will have a profound impact on the future of the Internet. Those of you who have IE5 already have this new technology, whether you know it or not. Those investing in Windows Xp and versions of Office beyond 2000 will also have it in many of their everyday Office products, such as Word and Excel.

This new technology came about as a result of the development of new Internet access devices and a need to standardise on how data is exchanged. This Chapter explains what this new technology is and why it had to come about - it is called XML.

The first big change - how we access the Internet
Today, most Internet access is via desktop computers. But recent technology has made possible many new devices capable of transferring information over the Internet - palm top computers, mobile phones, home telephone systems, TV boxes, talking car phones, etc. Some are capable of displaying only small amounts of information, some are purely aural devices, some, like the TV boxes, cannot as yet scroll text. (Ever wished you could when reading Teletext?) Some computer analysts claim that by 2002 (others by 2005) 70% of Internet access will be via these devices rather than via our desk-top PCs.

HTML, the standard web language for displaying web pages on PCs, will not be used for the new devices. HTML was never designed to cope with such diverse devices, so a new web language is required.

What is wrong with HTML?
Nothing! HTML has done a remarkably good job at popularising the growth of the WWW and all in a very short time. It was only in 1994, a bare six years ago at the time of writing, that today's 'old-hands' began to create web pages; probably just 2 - 3 years for the vast majority of Web authors.

HTML was a language designed to mark up web documents in a *simple* way. Today's needs are more demanding. Apart from all the new devices, web authors need DTP (desk top publishing), multi-media (animation, sound, music and videos in our web pages) especially with the advent of distance learning. Even `gif` and `jpeg` files leave much to be desired since they lose quality when resized. HTML cannot cope properly with such demands since it was never designed to handle them in the first place. Fudges have been attempted as is woefully obvious when viewing multi-media on many current web pages.

As with most products, HTML has come to the end of its 'best before' date. The demands of the world move on. It is not being developed any further, a new language is demanded.

The second big change - a standard data exchange
Of much greater significance is the fact that the Internet is fast becoming a major means for exchanging and sharing information. Information such as everyday letters, invoices, medical details, insurance details, sound, pictures, videos, book titles, newspaper, magazine and journal articles, ordering from our local supermarkets, banking, almost anything you can think of including radio

transmissions, TV material, on-line shopping. The Internet will be used more and more to transfer such data from one web site to another. Again a new language is demanded which can describe data more easily.

Let us take an example. Someone has a nasty accident and is taken unconscious to hospital. Ideally, the hospital will need that person's medical details from the GP and perhaps medical insurance details from an insurance company. The details will have to be entered into a hospital record for the patient.

Currently, the information will be in three different formats, each having been entered via some proprietary program. The GP will be using one program, the insurance company a second proprietary program and the hospital yet a third.

Eventually, the hospital will need to send back details to the GP and the insurance company. Again, someone will have to re-type the details into their own program.

Now, imagine if all three used the *same data format*. The data could now be sent over the Internet and simply dragged and dropped into the various local programs without any further human intervention (and the possible risk of incorrect typing). To do this would, of course, require some common or standard means of marking-up the original data which the three sites would have agreed to adopt. That is the sort of new language we need whereby any program can recognise the same set of data.

Sharing electronic information

Sharing electronic information has always been a problem and still is. How many times have you been unable to open an e-mail attachment? I use Excel but you send me a Lotus file. I send you a Word document but your version of Word is different. And what about the problem of data being held in different database programs. We seem to end up with something like this:


```
8BPS` ´ ` ` ` ` ` ` ` ` ˜ ` ` ´  ` ` ´  ` ˚ ` ˜ ` ` ` ` ` ` `  ¯ 8BI
M˜ é` ` ` ` ` x` ˜ ` ` ` ` H` H` ` ` ` ˆ Ú ˆ (ÿáÿâˆ ùˆ F˜ G˘ (˜ ü
` ˆ ` ` ` ` H` H` ` ` ` ˆ Øˆ (` ´ ` ` ` d` ` ` ` ` ` ˜ ˜ ˜ ` ` ` ` ´ ‘ÿÿÿÿ
ÿÿÿÿÿÿÿÿÿÿÿÿÿÿÿÿÿÿÿ˜ è` ` ` ` ÿÿÿÿÿÿÿÿÿÿÿÿÿÿÿÿÿÿÿÿÿÿÿÿÿ˜ è` `
` ` ÿÿÿÿÿÿÿÿÿÿÿÿÿÿÿÿÿÿÿÿÿÿÿÿÿ˜ è` ` 8BIM¯ ˚ ` ` ` ` ` ` ` Ł` ` ` ` ´
` ` ˆ @` ` ˆ @` ` ` ` 8BIM¯ fl` ` ` ` H` ` HLinoˆ Ł` ` mntrR
GB XYZ ¨ Î` ˆ `          ` ` ` 1` ` acspMSFT` ` ` ` IEC
sRGB` ` ` ` ` ` ` ` ` ` ` ` ` ` ` ` ` öÖ` ´ ` ` ` ` Ó-HP
```


The data can seldom be imported into a different program without having to ‘slap it around a bit’. To understand the problem, we need to go back to the Swinging 60s.

1960s

In the 1960s, it became possible to use computers for storing and displaying documents. It then became clear that *content* and *structure* were two separate issues which had to be addressed when storing documents electronically. Do you recognise the following?

```
TEN:The Future of the Internet - XMLThere is
a new development taking place which will
have a profound impact on the future of the
Internet. Those of you who have IE5 already
have this new technology, whether you know it
or not. Those investing in Windows Xp and
versions of Office beyond 2000 will also have
it in many of their everyday Office products,
such as Word and Excel.
```

It is first part of this chapter. It is the content without any structure. There are no line spaces before and after the paragraphs, no spacing before the headings. It is difficult to read. When computers store data, they not only have to store the content, but also how it is going to be displayed by a program, such as Word or Excel.

When entering data (a letter, memo, company reports, chapter of a book, a spreadsheet, an image, etc.) into a computer we have to use a proprietary program, such as Word for documents, PowerPoint for presentations, PhotoShop for images, Excel for spreadsheets. When we save our files for storage in our hard discs, not only the content but also the details of how it is to be displayed the next time it is opened have to be stored. Should you attempt to open a file in a program other than the one used to create it, that program will not be able to recognise the display codes. Hence the problem when trying to open, say, an Excel file using the PowerPoint program.

In fact, three concepts have been identified:

- *Content:* A paragraph of text ....
- *Formatting - presentational - style* as in Word or Excel
- *Descriptive information*

Latterly, people are becoming more concerned with how to *describe* content rather than just its style and structure. Life would become more simple, if there were one common standard for describing data. Then any program would be capable of recognising it.

Now suppose, just suppose, that such a standard existed? Well, it does, something called the eXtensible Markup Language (XML). The X in eXtensible is not a typing error. Let us see where and how this new language came from.

The General Markup Language - GML

The first working system to address the first two concepts (content and structure) was the GML language devised at IBM in the late 1960s. It was used to produce their technical documentation. Managing and creating vast documents is not trivial. Likewise, storing such data so that content and structure are preserved is not simple. Searching for and finding information is yet another problem.

For example, Boeing's 747 manual is some 150,000 pages. Suppose you need to find the specification of the bolt which holds on the engine. When many people are involved in writing the technical manual, some may name the bolt `bolt123`, another `123bolt`, others again `123-bolt`. It should be clear that some consistency in creating names needs to be enforced.

Jump 15 - 20 years to c.1984

By the 1980s, microtechnology had made its entrance and there was a proliferation of workstations used as local networks. There was a need to standardise the exchange of information between all the various network systems and their different operating systems. The American National Standards Institute (ANSI) had been established and had begun research into descriptive mark-up in 1978. The International Standards Organisation (ISO) joined the fray and produced the Standard General Markup Language (SGML) in 1984. It was based on IBM's GML.

Who uses SGML?

Large organisations which produce masses of documentation, such as the US Defense Department and the Association of American Publishers, could afford to introduce a single standard format for internal use. There were other requirements such as DocBook, for writing sets of books; the Text Encoding Initiative (TEI) for research, historical and lexicographical texts. Tim Berners-Lee turned to SGML when he wanted to develop a Web language - HTML.

What is SGML?

It is a *meta* language or template for defining other languages, such as TEI, MIL-STD (used by the Military) and HTML. Each language is different, thus TEI is not the same as HTML. It can be thought of as English grammar, a language used to write books, letters, memos and poems. Each one is different but each is based on the rules (the syntax) of English Grammar.

HTML

Tim Berners-Lee turned to SGML when he wanted to define a new language for Web browsers. But to understand SGML one has to be a guru. It requires extensive study, it is costly and it was overkill for creating web pages. Thus, HTML incorporated only some of the very simple features of SGML. More akin to the language of comics rather than Milton's "Paradise Lost".

The design goals for HTML were:

- it should be easy to learn and use
- it should concentrate on content and structure
- it was intended for academic documents, containing textual information and some basic structure (lists, headings, paragraphs and blockquotes) but nothing fancy, just the odd bold and italic

It did not describe the content and was never intended to do so.

What does all this mean?

Let us return to our main point. We have two parallel requirements. First, a language which is capable of *describing* data so that information can be shared over the Internet. Secondly, a new HTML for use with all the new Internet access devices. Do we go back to SGML? No, it is too complex. What is needed is a new language which:

- has 80% of the functionality of SGML but only 20% of its complexity
- is easy to learn and easy to use
- can describe its content

Enter XML.

XML

The next page shows an example of a pure XML document. See if you can work out what it is.

It describes the details about the books and hobbies of the authors Fred Jones and Evelyn Waugh. It is purely descriptive. Even a human being can read it and understand what it is all about. One of the design goals of XML is that it should be both computer and human readable.

The example can be typed into any editor or word processor and saved as a text only file with an `.xml` extension. That is all there is to it. The indentation is not necessary, it is used to make the document more human readable.

Being a simple text file, it can now be opened in almost any program, NotePad, Word, Excel. I even 'opened' it in PowerPoint. It was still readable! It can also be read and understood by humans, just as it stands. So in the worst case, if this was sent over the Internet it could be opened in a word processor and read rather than the unreadable version on page 98.

Many programs we use today are being made XML compatible so that such files can be handled effortlessly.

Indeed, there is already one such program, Internet Explorer version 5. The screen shot on page 104 is what the XML source code looked like when opened in IE5, (just for Fred Jones, not Evelyn Waugh).

```
<?xml version="1.0"?>
<authorslist>
<author>
  <authorname>Fred Jones</authorname>
  <books>
     <book>
        <title>Balham - Gateway to the
                       South</title>
        <isbn>142-384-8675</isbn>
        <cost>£5.99</cost>
     </book>
     <book>
       <title>My Day out in Bootle</title>
       <isbn>142-384-8765-9</isbn>
       <cost>£7.99</cost>
     </book>
   </books>
   <hobbies>
     <hobby> Acol Bridge - level Master
     </hobby>
     <hobby> Wimbledon: seeded number 156
             in 1997
     </hobby>
   </hobbies>
</author>
<author>
  <authorname>Evelyn Waugh</authorname>
  <books>
     <book>
        <title>Scoop</title>
        <isbn>1-123-45678-x</isbn>
        <cost>£5.99</cost>
     </book>
    ... etc ....
</author>
</authorslist>
```

Note how IE5 shows minus and plus signs. By clicking on a minus, it collapses the contents, by clicking on a plus sign the contents are expanded. Another useful feature is that if you have any errors, IE5 highlights them and tells you what sort of error your source contains. But, if it displays the content, then your XML document is correct.

```
  <?xml version="1.0" ?>
- <authorslist>
  - <author>
      <authorname>Fred Jones</authorname>
    - <books>
      + <book>
      - <book>
          <title>My Day out in Bootle</title>
          <isbn>142-384-8765-9</isbn>
          <cost>£7.99</cost>
        </book>
      </books>
    - <hobbies>
        <hobby>Acol Bridge - level Master</hobby>
        <hobby>Wimbledon: seeded number 156 in
          1997</hobby>
      </hobbies>
    </author>
  </authorslist>
```

I could even get IE5 to display it as a web page, see Figure 10.1:

The eXtensible Mark-up Language - XML

Like SGML, XML is a special language used to define other languages. It is in fact, a sub-set of SGML but one which is easier to use and more suited to Web developers. SGML is notoriously difficult, costly and complex, reserved for use by specialists.

XML has been used to define a new web language - eXtensible HTML - XHTML. Fortunately, most of the tags used in HTML still apply to XHTML. So there is little new to learn. Why do we need this new web language? Because HTML cannot cope with the new Internet devices, but XHTML can.

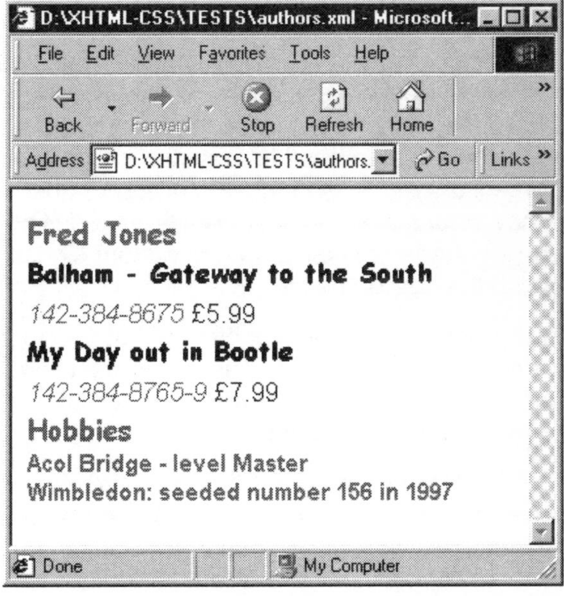

Figure 10.1 IE5 displaying an XML page

XML is not just one technology, it is the head of a family; children, cousins, aunts abound and doubtless new arrivals will appear in the future. XHTML is one of the members of the XML family and has access to the other members such as:

10: The Future

- SVG - scalable vector graphics
- SMIL - synchronised multi-media integrated language - pronounced 'smile'
- MathML - Mathematical markup language
- XSL - eXtensible style sheet language

SVG: There are two types of graphics, bitmap and vector. GIF, JPEG and PNG are bitmapped, that is, the files contain information about each pixel which makes up the image. A *vector* based format stores mathematical equations which describes how to redraw the image. A vector based file contains a collection of the lines, curves, and lines which are combined to draw the image. As such they are resolution independent which means that when resized they retain their original quality. In addition, the image can be made smaller or larger without significantly impacting on the size of the file.

One disadvantage of vector graphics is that they are not good at irregular images which cannot be described well by curves and lines. Thus, they are good for line art and illustrations but not for photographs.

At the present time, there is no standard for vector graphics on the Web. However, the W3C[1] aims to make SVG the standard which will make an impact on how graphics are defined on the Web. SVG is used for describing two-dimensional graphics in XML and will support three types of graphic objects: vector-based shapes, bitmaps and text.

SMIL: allows for co-ordination of multi-media elements, something which HTML cannot do.

---

[1] W3C is the World Wide Web Consortium responsible for standardising on web development. See `http://www.w3.org/` for details.

MathML allows equations and other mathematical figures to be included in web pages more easily than with HTML.

XLS: - the eXtensible Stylesheet Language - is an alternative style sheet language for styling XML documents. It is aimed at complex documentation projects. Most XHTML users will prefer to use CSS as the means for formatting their web pages.

All the above are features which many web designers have wanted for a long time, but which were not possible through HTML. They can all be incorporated easily into web pages built around XHTML. For example, an XML document can be put in the middle of an XHTML (and vice versa). Imagine how easy it would now be for search engines to find the hobbies of Fred Jones, the author. It would search on the descriptive tags and be able to provide exact details. At the present time, search engines would supply a list of everyone called Fred Jones, the butcher, the candlestick maker as well as the author. But with XML, it could easily find the cost of the book title "My Day Out in Bootle" by the author Fred Jones. Currently, search engines have no simple mechanism for this and hence the frustration we all have when trying to find very explicit information.

What about the standard data format? If you look at the XML document above, it is similar to the headings of a spreadsheet or database. If the document were sent as an e-mail attachment, it could be dragged and dropped into a spreadsheet which had the same headings and added to the bottom of a list of authors. This is the sort of thing which the new Office XML compliant programs will be able to do in the future.

Remember the accident example and how the hospital had to re-type all the data into their own program? Suppose the GP, the Insurance company and the hospital had all agreed on the same set of headings. The details could be dropped into the hospital patient records without all that typing. XML allows its users to select just the headings they want. Thus, the doctor could ask for all the medical headings (such as allergies, previous illnesses, blood groups, current medicines being taken, etc.). Just those details could be displayed on his palm top at the patient's bedside. The hospital's finance department would be able to ask just for the personal details and insurance data. This is where it is all going.

Some large organisations are already in the process of converting their existing data into XML. A mammoth task but one which will pay dividends within the next few years.

Even word documents have headings and the newspaper world is already using XML. For example, newspapers have major headings ("The Train That Ran On Time"), a summary section, a By-line, a picture, perhaps an insert, etc. Provided journalists keep to the same headings, their articles could now be sent over the Internet and collated by a newspaper program which is XML compliant.

This cannot be more than a taste of what XML is all about. We can summarise it as follows.

XML has been used to create the XHTML language. This language can incorporate all the other members of the XML family with ease, such as vector graphics, multi-media, etc. XML could be used to create a standard newspaper language, a medical records language, etc., so that its content can be selected and displayed easily. The documents will be sent over the Internet for speed and almost instant access.

Going back to our accident case and assuming that the patient has some sort of identification, it is possible that the ambulance crew could enter his details into a computer so that by the time he/she arrives at the hospital, all the records could have been transmitted via the Internet to the medical team (as well as the personnel staff). When the patient arrives, the medical staff will know his/her blood group, allergies, etc., and be in a position to respond accordingly.

Newspaper editors, TV news programmes, and so on could be sent reports from anywhere in the world and almost instantly slot them into the newspaper or news programme with the minimum of effort.

This means a mammoth investment. All concerned will need to know what headings to use and that is what is currently taking place. But it is all based on XML. New XML-compatible programs will come on the scene so that our data can be read with ease by many different programs.

We are in an interim period. Many large companies are already converting their existing HTML pages into XHTML and their data into XML. It is a large task. Whether or not all this will happen depends on many companies deciding to agree on common standards. There is a great deal of optimism, but a great deal of persuasion is required. Hopefully, we shall be hearing a lot more about XML in the not too distant future.

It is the beginning of the future. But for those who learn XML and XHTML, they will be ready to take advantage of the coming tide.

> "There is a tide in the affairs of men,
> Which taken at full flood, leads on to fortune;
> Omitted, all the voyage of their life is
> drowned in shallows and in miseries."

Brutus, Julius Caesar Act IV Sc. III

10: The Future

ELEVEN:

Legal and Moral Issues

The WWW provides a means for accessing information stored in various sites on the Internet. If I were to copy a picture from someone else's web page and use it, could I be prosecuted? If I obtain permission via e-mail from an author to use his or her material, would it stand up in a court of law? Could a college be prosecuted for what one of its students or staff members disseminates via its network?

The law is not yet clear about such issues. Indeed, laws governing information technology in general are few. Those which do are open to different interpretations. To give an example, in June, 1995, a judge of the State Supreme Court in Mineola, New York, ruled that a certain information provider was a *publisher* rather than a simple *distributor* of information. This distinction meant that it was sued for libel over some material which was posted to its financial bulletin board by an unknown user.

The judge drew the *fine* distinction because the company used humans and computerised systems to filter out objectionable material posted to its network. Not all information providers do this and, therefore, act along the lines of a book shop or library which simply distributes information. However, because this company screened messages, it was deemed to be acting as a publisher of information.

On the other hand, a recent High Court case brought by Demon Internet, one of the UK's largest service providers ruled as follows (taken from Metro July 11, 2001 by David Fickling under the headline: *Net firm wins Bulger ruling*):

> *"ISPs will escape prosecution if their web sites reveal the identity of James Bulger's killers, the High court ruled yesterday.*
>
> *However, they will have to remove any such information as soon as they find out about it, or risk prosecution.*
>
> *The ruling is being seen as a landmark decision which acknowledges that courts have little control over what happens in cyberspace.*
>
> ....
>
> *Internet law specialist Graham Smith said: "When ISPs are dealing with literally millions of messages and postings a day, it is simply not realistic to expect them to read every one to check if it's breaking the law."*

E-mail can remain on your system and come back to haunt you. You can delete it from your network computer (which you should do regularly). However, it may still reside on the network's archive system. "But they ought to delete out-dated files from their discs every so often!", you cry! So they should, but how many odds and ends have you got lying around unused and unwanted on your hard disc? We often wait until some extra space is required, before doing this chore. So do many system network people. Their discs are so vast, in terms of gigabytes[1], that some networks will not bother to delete files until some threshold is reached or extra space is required.

---

[1] giga = a thousand million, 10^9.

This means that some snoopy employer can rummage around employees' mail messages on the network, despite the fact that you have deleted your rude messages about your boss. Again, what legal action may employers take against employees who 'abuse' the company e-mail service? We have all read cases in the media. The moral is that *you* should be careful.

Just who is legally responsible for what is allowed on the Internet is a complex issue since there is no one body responsible for controlling what goes on to the Net. It is the responsibility of each separate network in the overall web of networks. Bearing in mind that these networks are owned by government, commercial, educational, private agencies, etc., and that they exist in over 69 countries each with its own laws, politics and customs, you can begin to see why it is so complex.

One university computer centre has had to apply guidelines, over 30 of them, for college users who put any kind of information onto the Net via the university network. Essentially, the college wishes to disassociate itself from any legal repercussions which could result from libellous material. Rightly so. Individual staff (or their heads of departments) have to sign a document making them responsible for any legal comeback. This has had a direct bearing on the conditions of employment. It certainly makes one think twice about what one puts up on the Web.

Morals

Porn, theft of information and of credit card details, breaking into computers (homes) reminds us of our unhappy society. They all exist on the Internet too, but the difference is the scale. It is not for one individual to change society, it is for all of us to change it.

Some people do use the Internet for their own dubious purposes, do not be surprised. The Internet makes it easy to gamble all day, create nail bombs and flick through porn. That is not quite what parents have in mind when buying a family computer. Essentially, the onus is on parents to protect their children from such material, since service providers are reluctant to censor material put up on their servers.

By using *Content Advisor* on your browser, you can screen out objectionable content by using industry-standard ratings that have been defined independently by the Platform for Internet Content Selection (PICS) committee.

There are dozens of filter programs, for about £20 - £30, which can be installed to block unwanted sites. Here are three highly recommended sites:

NetNanny (`www.netnanny.com`)
Cyber patrol (`www.cyberpatrol.com`)
SurfMonkey (`www.surfmonkey.com`).

Such programs work in one of two ways. Some have a huge list of unsuitable sites and block access to them if someone tries to type in their web addresses. Others scan the content of web sites for keywords and flesh tones. Neither method is perfect, however.

Another approach is offered by Ask Jeeves for Kids and Yahooligans which offer links only to safe sites.

`www.ajkids.com`
`www.yahooligans.com`

A similar approach is taken by the Atkidz ISP which connects your child to the Internet but allows access to 100,000 safe sites. It is free at the time of writing.

`www.atkidz.com`

For parents worried about the dangers of chat rooms, Childnet International, a charity, has compiled a list of guidelines to help parents. Try:

`www.childnet-int.org`

Legal Implications

Broadly speaking, there are at least three areas which affect what material is allowed on the Net:

- government *subsidies*, at least in some countries, pay for large sections of the Internet
- since the Internet is truly world wide, information will travel across national boundaries each with its own *export laws*
- when software is being carried from one place to another, intellectual rights and licence issues are raised

Subsidies

Whoever pays for a particular network has the right to say what that network will be used for. Therefore, I should not use my company's office computer to advertise my own personal business. If I have any doubt, then I ought to contact the network administrator and clarify the issue.

One simple case may help. A commercial company wanted to use a university teaching room which had micros linked to the Internet. The company, of course, would make a profit out of the courses to be offered, so would the university involved. The issue was that the network being used was an educational network which was not permitted to make commercial gains. Its use was restricted to research and education. The main point was that the particular university was not permitted to hand over its resources to a commercial organisation. Now if university staff were giving the courses and making all the profit for the college, that would have been a different matter.

When a site arranges for its Internet connection, it has to state whether the connection is to be used for commercial or educational purposes. If it is for educational use, then information tends to be routed over educational networks, such as JANET (see page 58). If its use is commercial, then the information is routed over private networks.

Export Laws

Exporting anything, even software, requires a licence. Some types of software are not covered or restricted, some are. Networking code and encryption code may well be restricted. In other words, being helpful to a colleague in another country by sending some program code could prove to be illegal.

Likewise, if the export of a supercomputer is not allowed by a certain country, then remote access to that computer from an outside country may be prohibited too. Network administrators have to be careful about who can be granted access rights to hardware at their sites. Could they be legally held responsible? That may have to be decided by the courts.

Property Rights

Copyright and patent laws vary from country to country. It may well be legal to allow a program to be copied within one country but a breach of law if it is sent outside. What can you do? If you give anything away on the Internet, find out to whom it belongs and get their permission. Be warned, it is not clear whether getting permission via an e-mail message may actually count as valid in a court of law.

Some software can be accessed via the Internet from public sources, for instance, operating system updates. These may be supplied free by the vendors but may well require a licence from the vendor if it is to be *used*. You could find yourself with a problem if you were to take and use this public information without obtaining a licence. Obtaining the software may well be legal, but using it may not.

Plagiarism or Research?

Finally, online plagiarism has become more common. It is simple to find 'essays' on the Web and pass them off as your own and is becoming a concern for universities.

Mind you, has this not been the way we have always worked. (I was not born with all knowledge. I have had to find what others have discovered in order to make it my own. I always thought this was called *research*, provided the sources were acknowledged.)

Why Cannot the Porn Merchants be caught?

Every web page has an address, so why is it not possible to go to the address and find the culprit? The short answer is that a web address is not like a house address but more like a mobile telephone number. The number (web site) can be contacted, but you have no idea where the site is physically located. Hence the mobile rings next to you on the train and the person is asked "Where are you?" and the inevitable reply is "I am on the train!".

Take this fictitious address:

`www.abc.com/pornpage.htm`

You may well know where the ABC company has its physical location. But its web server could be anywhere in the building, even some pokey little broom cupboard.

It is even possible for some employees to use an unused IP number of an organisation and set up a service from their home. Unless the actual porn files are found on a physical web server, the law cannot do much about it.

TWELVE

Useful References

Please note that these addresses were valid at the time of writing. Sites come and go or change their addresses.

http:// may be omitted and has been in some references.

1: Portals & Reference sites

Try About for general references mentioned on page 5:

`http://home.about.com/`

or for an A-Z listing of the above try:

`http://a-zlist.about.com/num.htm`

To find out how things work (mainly electronic and computers):

`www.howstuffworks.com`

How the Web is used today (page 6):

`http://www.cio.com/WebMaster/sem2_how.html`

For Web surveys (page 15):

`http://www.netcraft.com/survey/`

For street maps of the UK:

`http://www.streetmap.co.uk/`

For free web images:

`http://www.webshots.com/homepage.html`

2: Search Engines

For multi and meta search engine evaluations (page 46):

www.zdnet.com/searchiq/directory/multi.html

For those interested in receiving the free Search Engine Watch newsletter (by e-mail) and for many interesting articles about search tools in general:

http://searchenginewatch.com/

Some search tools:

Google: www.google.com

Alta Vista: www.altavista.com

Northern Light: www.northernlight.com

Yahoo!: www.yahoo.com
(Click the "UK only" box for sites specific to the UK)

Ask Jeeves - USA: www.askjeeves.com
Ask Jeeves - UK specific: www.ask.co.uk

Meta & Multi Search engines (page 46):

www.queryserver.com

http://vivisimo.com

3: Newsgroup Information

Search for a newsgroup via keywords (page 36):

http://groups.google.com/

List of all UK newsgroups (page 38):

www.usenet.org.uk

What is USENET (page 33):

www.faqs.org/faqs/usenet/what-is/part1/

Some groups of possible interest, but there are 40,000 more! You will need to access the following via your browser's newsreader.

uk.jobs.offered
uk.local.geordie
talk.environment
uk.sport.football.clubs
rec.arts.tv.uk.eastenders (or coronation-st)

4: For parents

Here are three highly recommended sites:

NetNanny	www.netnanny.com
Cyber patrol	www.cyberpatrol.com
SurfMonkey	www.surfmonkey.com

Ask Jeeves for Kids and *Yahooligans* offer links only to safe sites:

www.ajkids.com
www.yahooligans.com

The Atkidz ISP which connects your child to the Internet but allows access to 100,000 safe sites:

www.atkidz.com

Childnet International, a charity, has compiled a list of guidelines to help parents. Try:

www.childnet-int.org

5: Miscellaneous sites

JANET (page 57):

http://www.ja.net/

Newsgroup for HTML (page 34):

comp.infosystems.www.authoring.html

12: References

For encryption by Pretty Good Privacy (page 29):

http://www.pgpi.org/

http://web.mit.edu/network/pgp.html

For eGroups (page 28):

http://www.egroups.co.uk/

Glossary:

account — in order to gain access to a network, you need to register and be given an account.
A *network* account consists of your user identification and password as well as whatever access rights have been granted to you.
An *e-mail* account comprises an account name and an e-mail server address separated by an @ symbol.

address — either an e-mail address, so that messages can be sent directly to a person, or the site address of a network on the Internet.

backbone — any large, fast network system which connects a variety of smaller networks. JANET forms a backbone for the academic communities in the UK.

BBS — Bulletin Board System which became USENET. Today, more commonly known as *newsgroups* which allows anyone to post messages publicly.

bookmark or favourite — most browsers allow their users to keep a record of the address of a web page which they may wish to re-visit in the future. It saves the users having to re-type the address each time.

browsers — programs used to explore the World Wide Web. Internet Explorer and Netscape are among the most popular browser programs.

Glossary

chat rooms — a chat room provides its users with the ability to talk in real-time with each other while they are online. A chat room is software that allows a group of people to type in messages that are seen by everyone in the "room".

client — a program which extracts some service or information on your behalf from a server computer somewhere on a network. For example, a browser becomes a client when you click on a hypertext link to another web page.

directory — a search tool for finding web pages. The database, however, has been compiled by *humans* rather than computer programs.

DNS — Domain Name System which translates domain names into the numeric numbers used by the Internet Protocol (IP).

domain name — the address of a web server using names rather than the IP numbers.

dotted-quad — quaint term for the four numerical numbers separated by dots and used by the Internet addressing system.

e-mail — electronic mail messages. Text messages sent to anyone connected to the Internet.

e-mail address — a unique address used to forward e-mail messages to a specific computer on a network.

emoticon — see *smiley*.

encryption — a method of encoding data so that it cannot be read by unauthorised recipients.

extranet a private Internet which allows only authorised members of the public to view certain resources on a given network.

FAQ short for Frequently Asked Questions (rhymes with *back*). Users are encouraged to look through the list of answers before asking a question which may already have been answered.

firewall a security device to protect private networks from destructive forces such as offensive web sites and hackers.

flame an abusive attack against someone who has posted a newsgroup message to which someone violently objects. Flame wars erupt when others join in and keep repeatedly sending out their flames.

gif an image format which browsers use to display images such as logos and basic line drawings. It is really a technique for compressing the original image into a smaller file so that it can travel over the Internet more quickly.

home page the default page you see each time you call up your WWW browser. You can create your own home page or use someone else's. Also refers to the default web page sent by a web server if no web page has been specified in a URL.

HTML HyperText Mark-up Language is the language used to create pages of information on the WWW. Browsers read the HTML to find out how the page should be displayed and laid out on the screen. It is to be replaced by XHTML.

Glossary

http	the Hyper-Text Transfer Protocol is the standard protocol used extensively by Web servers to transfer information between networks over the Internet .
hypertext	text or images which contain a link to where further information is stored. By clicking on a hypertext, a new page is displayed.
hypertext-link	the Web address of where some further information is stored.
instant messaging	similar to e-mail, except that the recipient must be online in order to receive the message. The messages are not normally kept once the session has ended.
Internet	the physical means whereby information is sent via routers from one local network to another using special protocols.
intranet	a private Internet allowing only authorised employees to view an organisation's network resources.
IP	Internet Protocol, the rules by which web server addresses can be recognised and found.
ISP	Internet Service Providers. Companies allowing customers to use their Internet link, usually at a cost.
JANET	Joint Academic Network, a private, government funded network. All further and higher education organisations are connected to JANET as are all the research council institutions. JANET has a Connection Policy which defines who can connect to the network and an Acceptable Use Policy defining what it can be used for.

jpeg	an image format used by browsers to display images of a photographic nature. It is really a technique for compressing the original image into a smaller file so that it can travel over the Internet more quickly.
LAN	Local Area Network, a collection of computers which can communicate with each other in a local vicinity such as a building.
login	the process of typing in your user name and password to gain access to a network on which you have an account.
lurker	someone who reads newsgroups mail but who does not wish to add to the conference/discussion.
meta-search engine	a search tool which provides links to your search keywords from a variety of individual search engines and directories.
MIME	Multipurpose Internet Mail Extensions, a method of encoding files so that not only text but images, sound and videos can be sent via e-mail.
modem	MOdulator-DEModulator, a device which allows data to be transferred between computers via the telephone system.
multi-media	not just text but also images, sound and video.
network administrator	each network has its own network systems administrator or manager. It is the role of this person to see to the smooth running of the network and to provide assistance to all users. In many cases, the manager is responsible for the security of the network

and for monitoring what is allowed to be put up on the network for access by other users.

newsgroup a message area or forum for USENET relating to a defined subject matter.

newsreader a program which allows news from newsgroups to be read or posted.

on-line being physically connected to one's LAN or ISP network. When the connection is broken, one is said to be *off-line*.

packet data transmitted over the Internet are broken into smaller packets, usually about 1500 characters. They have to be re-assembled at the other end.

pixel short for picture element. PC screens are made up of thousands of pixels, each containing one colour. They are square but at the correct resolution we do not see the individual squares. A simple example is shown on page 132.

png another web based image format, seldom used. It was meant to replace the gif format.

post to send a message to a conference or newsgroup.

protocol standards or rules which define how information is passed between computers.

real time events, such as replying to a message, obtaining data from a database, which occur instantly with no delay time involved.

router a computer which transfers data between two networks which use the same protocols.

	It forms the main backbone of the Internet. Without routers, the Internet could not exist.
search engines	Commercial organisations, such as Alta Vista, Northern Light. They form a data base of web pages so that when a user requests web pages for a particular topic, the data base is searched and the user is supplied with a list of sites and web titles which match the original query. They differ from *directories* since the web pages are collated by computer programs rather than humans.
server	a computer, such as a web server or e-mail server, which stores information. When a client, such as a browser or e-mail program requests information, the server handles that request.
service provider	an organisation, either academic or commercial, which allows other computers to access the Internet through its own network. Frequently called Internet Service Providers (ISP).
shareware	software which you can try out before you buy it. If you like it, you register with the producer and pay a fee.
SMS	short message service. See text messaging.
site	any of the local area networks which comprise the Internet. Today, web pages are confusingly called a web site.
smiley	smiling faces consisting of ASCII characters used in e-mail and similar messages to denote joy or sadness. Turn the page

	sideways and see if you can make these out. :-(:-) Some use a semi-colon to denote a wink ;-) Also called an *emoticon* in text messaging parlance.
subscribe	to join a discussion group by being added to its mailing list.
system manager	see network administrator.
TCP	Transmission Control Protocol, the system which breaks up data into smaller *packets* for transmission over the Net. The packets have to be re-assembled at the receiving end.
text messaging	the use of mobiles to send text messages to other users. Beloved by teenagers and, more recently, commercial organisations to send out their promotions. Also known as short message service (SMS).
threads	a series of postings about a particular discussion or conference. There is the initial message, which starts the whole discussion going, and the threads which form part of the subsequent discussion.
URL	Uniform (or Universal) Resource Locator. The method of specifying the location of resources on the Internet. Used mainly with www.
USENET	USErs' NETwork. The group of systems which exchange 'news'. Now more commonly known as newsgroups.
WAN	Wide Area Network. A network which may be national or global in extent, as opposed

to a local area network.

Web masters A new job title for people in organisations who are responsible for maintaining all the web pages on the web server of that institution. In some cases, they also check the quality of the material as well as looking for any breach of a legal nature.

WWW short for World Wide Web.

XHTML eXtensible HTML: the new languages for creating web pages. It is set to supersede HTML which is not being developed any further.

XML eXtensible mark-up language. The new web language used to create XHTML and to standardise on how data is to be exchanged over the Internet.

Glossary

The following shows the pixels which make up the image. It has been blown up, hence the blurring. You should be able to see the square pixels, the picture elements.

Here is the original:

Please note: **f** after a page reference indicates **f**ollowing pages.

INDEX

Index

Index